The Years and Beyond

Inspirational Poetry

William Furr

authorHOUSE™

1663 Liberty Drive, Suite 200
Bloomington, Indiana 47403
(800) 839-8640
www.AuthorHouse.com

First published by AuthorHouse 01/09/06

ISBN: 1-4208-7053-X (sc)

Library of Congress Control Number: 2005906586

Printed in the United States of America
Bloomington, Indiana

This book is printed on acid-free paper.

Table of Contents

THIS BOOK IS DEDICATED TO

MY BELOVED COUNTRY, AMERICA—

THE GREATEST LAND ON EARTH

From a letter from former U.S. president,
GEORGE BUSH:

Your poem is a moving tribute to those brave Americans who gave their lives in defense of our precious freedom and this land we all love. We can never repay the debt of gratitude we owe them, but we can, and must, ensure their heroic legacy is never forgotten. Your poem eloquently does just that.
Thank you for your kindness in sharing it with me. God bless you and God bless America.

-GEORGE BUSH
June 6, 1989

From the Congressional Records-Extensions of Remarks,
January 7, 1991

SALUTE TO THE HEROES
HON. G. V. (*Sonny*) MONTGOMERY
OF MISSISSIPPI
IN THE HOUSE OF REPRESENTATIVES
(*Monday, January 7, 1991*)

MR. MONTGOMERY. MR. SPEAKER, one of my constituents, MR. BILL FURR, JR., of Columbus, MS, recently sent to me an eloquent and poignant expression of his feelings about America's heroes—our veterans—and their immeasurable sacrifices in the name of freedom.
In the following poem, MR. FURR also captures the spirit and tenacity of America and its vigilance regarding justice and individual rights. By commemorating courage and loss, he reminds us why we remain strong and secure.
I am pleased to share MR. FURR'S stirring words with my colleagues:

SALUTE TO THE HEROES

The air is cool; the fiery dawn of a new day
starts to break the far horizon. The wild chirp
of the fowl echoes through a green carpet laid
out to border long rows of white marble crosses.

All at once the blare of a lone bugler
Drowns out the cries of the wilds.
The flag is being raised; the blood spilt
Upon the grass of the free t'was sacrificed
Not in vain, not in boastful circles,
But in glory and honor.

Silence!!!

There comes upon the land
A new dawn day;
A freshness that cannot be marred
By idle, careless say—

A day of honor and glory,
A day of sharing and give,
A day to be remembered
For what our young boys did!
The women of American began to lay the
wreaths and flowers upon the marble
tombstones. The results of hard work and
sacrifices have made many a mother weep
uncontrollably upon her young son's grave. It
was just too much for them to bear upon
seeing their precious boys lying so still in that
cold silent state of not answering back.

1

Do not forget us, oh, God,
Thou faithful servants passed;
We died not in shame
But in thy holy tasks—

The eagle still flies high
Over the land that you set free
With all our strength and courage
We died to honor thee!

From small humble villages
To large dwelling towns
You are but our Lord;
You'll never let us down

If we hold your truths
And Christlike righteous ways,
The countries of thine earth
Shall respect us in our days

Listen!!

On yon distant hill
A staunch bugler blares;
Sounding out a warning
To every foreign dare—

For nations rise and nations fall.
T'was reflected in thy script;
What lies ahead of soaring storms
America will come to grip!

Oh, the brave and the free
Must come to you and say
"Lord, thou faithful father
Please guard us in our play."
For we as small young children

Laid our souls to rest
Upon thy golden throne
With every sin confessed

The country 'tis much stronger
Than ever she was before.
Oh! keep her with thy will
Throughout our struggling chores!
How much time we've spent on emphasizing
the true qualities in life; always stressing the
positive values of living in a free nation where
the worth of a single individual is paramount.
God, make us mindful of what a tremendous
price our founding fathers paid in establishing
a great nation like America!

Amen!! and Amen!!

The service has now ended
The people go their way,
For America was made for working
And not for weeping say—

The columns now have marched
Upon eternity's sky
Guarding us by day
In God's watchful eye.

The flag colors flow so brightly
Blowing in the breeze,
For many a heavenly angel
Got down upon their knees—

In that white-marked landscape
Where many a young man lies
To wait for Christ to come
And go where He resides!!!

ETERNAL WORKS

The bird that flies with lofty wings
And daisies along life's way
And fields of lush, rich, ripe corn
And children a' playing and gay.
All are brought here by the One
Who lifted His sanctified hand
And caused the mighty, boundless deep
To bring forth love and man!

Those infinite stars in heaven entrenched
And waves that pound some sea
And mountains that bear the greatest work
Are all for us to see.
For songs the air brings by our way
With melodies which sooth and sing
Are all the product of His love
God! Great God! Our King!

We poets old who toil by rhyme
And all our lyrics past
Which expound God's greatest, wonderous love
Hath all drunk from God's glass.
For God Almighty hath given us pens
And paper straight from His scroll
And miles and miles of loving words
To tell man of His goal!

That burning sun entrenched in space
With millions of warming rays
And raindrops as God's infinite stars
And flowers that grow in May
All t'wer brought here by the One
Who caused the mighty deep
To spew forth life from out His toil
And bless His world with peace!

Those infinite rhymes we mortals make
That find their place in time
Upon God's greatest, sacred book
Stand throughout all time.
And upon His truths we find our place
Through courts and judgement sent
Throughout all time and righteous works
Before God's firmament!

As years and time find each our lives
Drawing on what we choose
Upon God's grand, eternal love
And if, indeed, abused.
We shall reap our daily works
Upon God's sacred throne
And bear to light our failing lives
Throughout eternity's home!

As numerous as the sifting sands
Upon some seashore fair
God's never-ending love for us
Hath all His sacred care.
For He the Greatest One of All
Hath sent His Righteous Son
To draw our souls into His flock
And save us every one!

God's moving hand I'm told, it seems,
Draws throughout all time
Upon His Greatest, Wonderous Book
And places each our rhymes.
For all the love we spend for Christ
Doth place our eternal souls
Into God's grand, wonderous page
And find our heavenly goal!!!

DESTINED

I have not finished the course.
I have not won the race.
For the day never ends its warmth
As I "burn" the pages in haste.

The ink that I pen so freely
T-was made from God's own rain
And flows like an ever-ending river
Approaching the shores of fame.

As lyrics come from the dark night,
The heavens open up their arms
To receive those "hallowed" blessed sonnets
And protect them from all earth's harm.

For God hath given His blessings
And bestowed upon me His gifts
To rhyme the morning's fresh dew drops
And calm the reader's riffs!!!

BEHOLD!

The waves at sea, this great blue sky
And endless shores of sand
And all those mighty dreams Earth bore
Show great God's eternal hand.
Far beyond time's realm in place and space
And just beyond our flesh
A never-ending love tis forth
From out God's endless bless!

The stars that shine and fill our souls
Twinkle and seemingly prance
Upon God's forever timeless grace
From out His heavenly stance.
And shining jewels which show the face
Of grand and loving dreams
Tis all, henceforth, God's greatest work
Aside from Christ, our King!

Fresh laden are His fields and ripe
Are food for thought today,
And for the weary souls at bay
Some strength along life's way.
For all god's seed hath roots entrenched
In firm and ample soil;
No one shall starve for lack of love.
No one shall reap the spoils!

As grand as towers above some land
Are pines and oaks in height,
And far as the fartherest eye can see
Are moonbeams through the night.
For all God's land t'was born of grace
No mortal can take its place,
And all God's love tis meant for us
Along our vulnerable haste!

Earth's canyons deep with running brooks
And deer along their rim,
And all those little "sparks" of life
Are God's own beautiful gems.
And those skies above this bountiful earth
Soar to His great place
For all are wrought with doves and love
From out God's endless grace!

As deserts gleam with "prickle" brush
And sands are white and gray
And boulders by the ton are strewn
Along life's credible way.
We humans marvel at wonderous signs
From out this earth we cry
"Oh, make us, Lord, in all accord
Believers by the eye!"

As oceans roll in grand array
And "breakers" pound the sands
Of islands far removed from sight,
We marvel at God's plan
And humble little creatures move
Along their brief short way.
They all t'wer meant in present tense
To glorify our stay!

Those icy plains of chilling cold
Which adorn a snow-capped land
Where all the world tis frozen turf
And all tis white and grand.
There shows a never-ending God
Who sanctified this life
All cuddled close by His brush strokes
And resting throughout His night!

From whales at sea all swimming free
To miles of endless sage
From all earth's bountiful crops of corn
And honey by life's way,
There shows God's eternal, infinite plan
A'front for all to see.
The sign could be no plainer than
Some robin in some tree!

Those little candle flies at night
That light this earth so right
And all those shining, innocent eyes
Carass our hearts so light.
We all are products of His age;
We all are there to see.
Behold God's great, eternal plan
Tis meant for you and me!

Time's mighty hills which rise into
God's skies above earth's crest
And all those lush green valley floors
Doth show His infinite best.
As all the rich, ripe harvest fields
Abundent throughout this land,
They show God's never-ending love
In tune with angel bands.

We mortals in our follies waste
And strive in search of love
While in this time God's forever grace
Tis free from heaven above
And all those tender, eternal signs
Doth show His rapturous love,
For all who take the cross with Him
And strive for "up above"!

We rue our toils in deed and work
And tire by endless miles,
But far beyond this place called earth
Are angels with loving smiles.
For Christians who had their "brute" of things
And made life's eternal page,
Their role shall be a gracious one
Upon God's endless stage!

We poets strive into God's night
And draw His dreams to live
Of "Great Jehovah" who loved us so
And gave us bread to live.
For night by day and through this earth
Our rhyme shall be His song
Of man and earth and forever worth
Of love and God's great home!

As kingdoms of some ruling sect
Decree their laws today
And streets are filled with "wares" of man
Throughout life's short-lived stay,
There tis a greater gift than this
And worth forever more—
There tis the gift of life around
God's earth and world galore!

As poets in their "tottering" rhymes
Expound their thoughts at bay
And scholars of the greatest minds
Predict our every day,
There is a higher power true
A force from out this rhyme—
There tis God's eternal, lasting love
True and grand and kind!

The nations of this earth in worth
Fight on throughout their muck,
And kingdoms born of greed and deed
Lie trampled in time's dirt.
As cities rise into the skies
And mankind draws His pain,
There tis another rich-ripe land
Far from this grief and rain!

There is a wonderful, glorious one
Who calls this land His own—
Another one who gave His all
And left us for His home.
Far beyond this earth of "scented myrrh"
There lies a better grace.
It is our Christ with open arms
To greet us in His place!

God gives His children "lovingness"
And saves throughout their rhymes
And comforts all who ask of Him
For bread and life in time.
For all who seek eternal wealth
Which lies amid the skies
They shall find their "treasured gold"
In love and never die!

The rhyme doth wear the poet down
And age doth creep to flesh,
And years by years and lots of tears
Are strewn throughout our quest.
But all the dreamer hath to do
Tis gaze into the night,
Then all the lasting words from God
Shall come into our sight!

This earth in all its values' worth
Cannot match love from Christ,
And all the emeralds in the hills
Cannot bring joy to write.
For as the scholar draws unto
Some "tattered" sheet of page,
He shall find for all he knew
T'was small by God's own gauge!

As earth with all its beauty hence
Doth turn throughout all time
And seasons come and seasons go
And poets try their rhymes,
The grace brought forth from out God's love
Brings sinners to His throne—
For all who ask for saving grace
Shall find their rightful own!

The devil holds the keys to hell
And "beams" of deathly wage
And greets each sinner by their wails
To hot and endless days.
For all we know he may be near
And closer than we think
Tis is for poets who hold the cross
To cast him from their ink!

"Great Gabriel" in the highest cloud
Rehearses for that day
When he shall sound God's "heralds high"
And charge into earth's way.
For all we know He may be far
Or closer than we think—
No one shall know God's greatest time
Or know what He does think!

The years hath passed upon our flesh
And the "toll" of earth hath taken
And our brows are lined with pain and grief
For we tremble and are awakened.
We stare at earth and all its seas
And dream of those long miles
Wherein we wore our bodies frail
And reminisce when we were child!

God grants this space for this poor soul
Why rhymes into His night
And draws His thoughts upon God's page
His prolific rhymes to write.
We dream of timeless, beautiful days
Of earth when we were young
And call upon our Christ, our King
When all our work tis done!

As time doth quench the breath from us
To close our bodies down
And give the soil its fertile worth
And leave this earth, our town,
We Christians in all our joyful love
Shall greet God's gates of home
And draw on what we gave to Him
Upon His eternal throne!

Far from out this sphere in time and place
Which lies amid God's stars
This earth in all its rhythmic grace
Says forth "How great Thou art."
And all those eternal, timeless lights
From out God's endless bless,
We all shall greet His infinite rhyme
And sanctify the rest!!!

TIMELESS MASTER

It has been said that "the world is not run by thought, nor by imagination, but by opinion." May I be so bold as to insert into this "provocative hypothesis" that the world is not run by thought, not by imagination, and not by opinion. Rather, it is run by the "prolifical desires" of a force that is eternal and never ending—by a ceaseless, timeless Master who knows all, is all, and loves all.

Our God draws each and every charitable word and thought from out our frail-like minds and hearts. He cares for us so much that He hath charged us with this world into which He hath created for us to "act" out with our own "grand finale." He draws into His "books of life" our credits, our liabilities, and our never-ceasing charges of endless intentions which he hath accumulated throughout our brief occupancy upon this "spherical earth mass," floating in His eternal everlasting space.

May God Almighty have mercy on us and may His "Esteemed Son," Jesus Christ, forgive us our sins as we "piddle away" our stay upon this earth with "pettiness" and "ill-advised contemplation." Though the hour be late upon our earthly bodies, His love for us is unrelenting and ceaseless.

One day we shall leave our little "secluded domain" which we have wrapped ourselves into and shut out the real true virtues of love and compassionate existence. We, then, shall realize that our world was not "run by thought, imagination, or by opinion" but by our timeless, endless "Supreme God" who has loved us so very much to have given us His Own Begotten Son and hath included us into His eternal grand plan. For only then it shall be all too late to stop and re-write our tragic acting of his charitable scripts... .

OUT WITH THE GOLDEN ROD

The crust of fall tis in the air
As leaves turn born in cool dry days—
As autumn inverts the quieter pace
And summer tis gone to gayer ways—
The scent of the harvest covers Earth's crest
And love settles down while cupid's heart throbs—
For God and man and the kingdom's grand feast
Make room for the spectacular golden rod!

Less Earth in its imperfective, tantalizing ways
Holds back its mirth and fresh dew scent—
The golden rod comes forth by the "wing"
While archangels play their gracious intent—
The picturesque field in all her charm
Shan't slow the pace of this "vivacious" weed—
The drama plays forth the act in hand
And frolics through fall with decisive speed!

The wind blows cool from the gray, far north
As man and beast doth find their place—
With this harvest of rich, ripe "songs"
And stock those foods in quicken pace—
The yellower fields play out their games
From time eternal to present "sighs"—
We gaze upon God's golden rod
With awe and love and envious eyes!

The day's soft touch of wind and breeze
Shall bring forth those who passed it by—
The workers, the laborer, and "penning" me
And ask the weed—what avails—thy???
And wait in all our rarity group
For answer while the minutes pace—
But faith and heavens doth forth consume
The time, while snow christens Earth's face!

William Furr

The hill tis covered with ice and chill
And little small rabbits with awesome fears
Hide among the frozen weeds
While God sheds His cooler tears—
The "pious" plant that took Earth's stage
Of nature's "finale"—curtains—rise—
Has weathered upon this froze land
And winter has come with pomp and style!

The Earth tis covered with white and snow
As sleigh bells make their merry way
Upon the land where children's fun
Interrupts the problems that "prod" our day—
And some have said that once a year
God dips His "brush" and colors His sod
And brings man tidings of truth and peace
To Earth!—with His beautiful golden rod!!!

WINDOW

I see the world from beyond my window
As though one distant plain
Where sapiens choose paths to tread
Through sleet and fire and fain.
Whether he be the good, righteous few
Or the devious with cunning intent,
The pane reflects the starlight
Of a world hell-torn and bent!

I see the world from beyond my window
Where little small crickets chirp
Where dogwoods blossom every year
And birds and animals flirt!
Where God and man and starlight
And all time's trajectory beams
To light the path of pen strokes
So fools, as I, can dream!

IN THE NIGHT
(To Emily—Died 1886)

I feel your vibrations strongly,
Sweat is pouring from my palms,
Fires have been lit in my soul
Realizing thy virgin charms.

Why stay thee so far away?
So far, far away in time.
Come alive, alert, my youthful lass,
And sing with me a rhyme.

Tell my soul the troubles you face
And mountains that you shall climb.
Come heartfully, oh, my girl so sweet
And be thou only mine!

Emboss your script upon my frame
Instill in me thou kind.
Tell me, darling of daring thoughts
Love undoubtedly blinds!

In the night a'fright at last, my lass,
I see your ghost once more.
Why goest thou to higher places
That cheat death at it's score?

Yes, in the night I write of ghastly script
Sonnets gushing from my heart
Of wars, men, and poetic lines
Of romances I never will start!

MY MONA BY THE BROOK
(Died 1765)

Upon some radiant dandelions
At the edge of a cold, running stream,
I laid all my soul aside
For flowers and my queen.

I laid her down by the brook's soft song
And whispered in her sweet ear,
"My Mona, my Mona, where have you gone?"
But no voice was I ever to hear.

For evening fell upon the quiet still woods
And dark shadows covered her fair.
Oh, Mona, my Mona, where have you, Lass, gone?
But all that t'was heard t'was the air.

But her quietness t'was prevalent that warm summer's night
As the woods called their tunes by her side.
Oh, Mona, oh, Mona, where art thou, our Lass
But our Mona just lay where she died.

A sadness charged forth into my bitter heart
As my Mona just lay by my chest.
The deer in the wilds and God's stars in His sky
Adorned my poor Mona at rest.

All her beauty t'was whisked towards the sky
With her flowers in her hair golden and long.
Oh, Mona, my Mona, where art thou be, Lass ???
But my Mona was dead and was gone.

As those flowers that sprang forth in glorious delight
And as the clear, cold brook ran on,
I cried my eyes as I wept by her side
For my sweet Mona had gone to her home.

The world keeps on turning in God's eternal role
And His skies are a crystallizing blue.
My dear Mona has gone to a far away land
Where God and the Christ Child are two.

Earth's woods are still there and those flowers still grow
As the seasons pass swiftly along.
My Lass, my Mona, God please be so kind
And give Mona a brook by her home.

WONDERMENT OF DISCOVERY
(A fable)

Upon some ruin the scholar digs
From out Earth's distant past
Yearning what the soil doth hold
And bring to light at last
A priceless treasure throughout the span
All hidden and tucked away
And bring to present a fleeting verse
Of past men in their lay!

He digs and digs with dirty hands
And wished the soil holds true
That grandest, beautiful, loving cup
Whence some man drank into.
But, lest he find the shallows verse
All gone in time's decay
And all the tears throughout those years
Of passed men gone away!

As darkness falls upon the ruin
He fires and kindles flame
To warm his soul throughout the night
And soothe his hands in pain.
For all the toils he strived by day
And all his labors spent
Hath not found that loving cup
Throughout his just intent!

As morning breaks from out the plain
The scholar starts anew
And digs and digs and hauls away
Those stones from distant view.
And, as he mires into the pit
He searches mad and bold
To find that sacred loving cup
And claim his long-sought goal!

William Furr

As time and scholar chip away
Into that dimming past,
He strikes a rim with broken trim
And reaches out to grasp.
But, nay, tis only but a stone
A long lost castaway
Some native carved hence years ago
And left it by the way!

As weeks and weeks turn into months,
The digger draws a clue
He shall not find that loving cup
Whence some man drank into.
For as he crawls up from the hole
That pit he'd dug in time,
His eyes were red with sorrow
His hopes were all unwinded!

As time and scholar travel
The long road back toward home,
The digger stops to wonder
What made the effort wrong.
For all that soil he lifted
From out time's dimly pit
Had not one ounce of treasure
Throughout his efforts spent!

The scholar packs his shovel
And spade and whiskbroom, too;
He looks around the internment
At all he dug into.
And as he loads his burden
Upon his lagging frame,
He spies a golden "glitter"
From out the night's cold rain!!

He reaches down to grasp that
For which he toiled in vain
And all at once he sees it
That loving cup so plain.
And as he draws his treasure
Into his roughened hands,
He thanks all time eternal
For all the luck at hand!

A story as this lonely
Tale of distant past
And of a scholar probing
And searching for that glass
Doth bring to mind our pleasure
As we behold that cup
And of the timely pleasure
Of all those men it supped!

A fable as this story,
A tale of distant lay,
All holds the keys to pleasure
As we doth read away
And of the lonely scholar
From out his deepened pit
Of joy from out the sorrow
Through time's own wonderment!

LAST OF THE LIGHT

One day I shall see the last of the light
As if some vulture blew out its flame
As if some darkened curtain covered
My eyes, in tears, all winched with pain.
For deep beneath the water's tide
My soul shall float to transit home
And find its rightful, deeded birth
Upon time's forever eternal song!

One day I shall see the last of the light
That eerie glare of crimson beam
That covers this earth in dawn's sweet song
Upon God's lasting, forever sting.
And, lo! My journey beneath the tide
Shall consume all grief and aging worth
And cast my songs upon the wind
That chills those waters and moves the surf!

One day I shall see the last of the light
Some God drawn in his pensive songs
And bathed His glories each their own
With love and toil and pitiful wrongs.
For time, oh, time which finally wins
Those battles upon life's memorable stage
Shall follow my bones to forever worth
And cover my breast with scented sage!

One day I shall see the last of the light
Upon that hill with stone and chill
And fury of the storm's death march
Into God's lasting eternal will.
And, lo, His rightful, gracious faith
Shall follow some new slave in his work
And sing a song of tranquil promise
Upon a sea of slaves and serfs!

My last, faint glimpse of fading beam
Hath all but turned its rays away
From err my toils and garnered songs
To highs as angels wing their way.
For time that allusive, intangible thing,
Hath all but closed its books of free
And draw those charges against my heart
To carry me on and forever be!!!

AMERICA, OUR AMERICA

America, our America
All glory sent from God
With mountains which doth rise away
Against her golden rod
And rivers which do wind their way
Upon her beaming face
Ah, that tis where our hearts doth lie
By her own beautiful grace!

Oh, America, our America,
Give us thy freedom's wealth
Upon thy brilliant glowing skies
With angels thy hath slept
And make us each who plod thy soil
More grateful and more bold
Oh, give us each thy freedom's song
To carry in our souls!

America, our America,
Our land of freedom's song
With cities that doth rise away
Against her glorious own
With valleys meant for roaming
And forests lush and green
Our America, our beautiful America,
We sing as freedom rings!

Oh, America, our America,
We proudly wave thy on
Upon thy endless shores we tread
And in our loving homes
As we exalt thy wonders
We, each, hath praised thy name
For giving us all thy glories
We shall guard thy fame!

America, our America,
Our land that shall forth last
She hath drawn all her boundaries
From out her noble past
And with each breath she takes
She carries hearts and souls
Into her loving bosom
And places in her scroll

Oh, America, our America,
We want to live with thee
God's greatest home of freedom's stripes
Across His boundless sea.
With all thy bells of freedom
And with a loving song
We, each, hath placed our beings
Upon thy golden throne!

America, our America,
God's land of children's sighs
From old folk by her meadows
To newborn babies' cries.
We, all, must take her challenge
And plod her endless turf
Towards freedom's grand own wonders
From out our country's worth!

Oh, America, our America,
You stand so grand and tall
Amist God's endless skylines
Your glories move us all.
And through thy rapturous brilliance
Our hearts are moved by thee
Oh, give us each thy freedoms
And keep us strong and free!

As time and America's calling
Hath drawn from God's on grace
We, each, hath seen her wonders
Before her loving face.
For, we who share those freedoms
We, all, hath placed our hearts
Into her saving kingdom
Where all men find their part!

Oh, America, our America,
God's own grand spacious home
Where liberty hath no lacking
Where freedom moves us on.
And in thy wonderous glories
We, each, hath taken thy hand
And placed our souls and beings
Into God's American land!

THIS DAY AND BEYOND

This day and beyond
Amid the thunderous roar
In blacken, death-like skies
Through whence the fury tore—
There t'was thrown a challenge
To each of us who call
Our blessed, sacred nation
God's greatest best of all!

On that memorable morning
Among the pools of red
Through burned-out ships that lay
Are men and women—our dead.
By prophecy in some scripture
God's will shall forth be done
And all our hearts and cares
Shall find the battle's won!

In war and conflicts challenge
As smoke doth clear the scene
As men and women lay still
Amid the enemy's sting,
Our nation, our blessed country,
Hath opened up its soul
And bled its sacred teardrops
Upon God's golden scroll!

As darkness starts to fade
By dawn's dim, creeping light,
The battle hath just begun
As America and soldiers fight.
For all our firm resolve
We each hath drawn in place
Shall triumph in God's end
And find its rightful faith!

As we bid them well
Our soldiers march to war
As children spread their daisies
Before our nation's door.
Our best, our loving all,
Hath commenced to fight for home
And right the devil's rue
And move our nation on!

In fleeting days as this
As tears and heartaches fly
Before time's great hereafter,
We carry our nation's pride
And bear out God's great will.
His script He penned in hand
And give Him all our hearts
And fight on Normandy's sand!

As we love our nation
And children go to school
As preachers draw God's flocks
Into Christ's bleeding wound,
Our hearts and all our minds
Shall be right there with those—
Who gave their lives away
For country and for soul!!

This day and beyond
As blood flows from the fight
As men and women go off
To stand up for what's right,
Our prayers and every thought
Shall follow them on to quest
And find their peaceful solace
And be God's greatest best!

As we love our country
And doves soar high above
As tears flow down the cheeks
Of those who lost their loved,
God's hand shall rightly hold
We each and lead us fair
Into His great hereafter
And comfort all our cares!

In war and pressing times
As darkness covers Earth
As tanks and guns fight on
Throughout Earth's fragile turf,
We lest hold each to truths
To all what God hath said
And raise our prayer to Him
Before our fallen dead!

As we give our hearts
To those of us who cry
For each lost cherished member
God gave His Son to die
And through our bleakest battles
God gave us all His love
To draw us close to Him
And triumph high above!

This day and beyond
As tears flow from the rage
As men and women give
Their lives in battle's wage
We each look toward our God
And His own Greatest Son
And give our hearts to Him
To collect what peace hath won!

SPILL OF LIFE

As we stand upon this aging earth
We embrace a celestial sea
Of millions and billions of endless lights
Given in ecstasy.
We gaze at God's own righteous signs
Whence come His starlit nights
And draw upon our longing quests
To see Him in our sight!

As mortals, we, the chosen lot
Hath scarce to word our rhymes
For from out God's boundless, eternal deep
He grants the sands of time
And brought unto His beautiful bliss
His loving, caring best
To sanctify His worldly works
And grant eternal rest!

We men of planet earth hath bore
Those trails of bountiful greed
And cast away our Biblical lore
In down-right disbelief.
We pluck earth's thorn from out our flesh
Upon our mournful cries
And blame it all on nature's deeds
And drown in our lies!

As centuries past hold dear to those
Who left their bodies nigh
As procession lines hath all abound
With tears and sobs and whys??
We less take note of past gone text
Which hold those keys of old
And draw our spirits once again
Into God's lordly fold!

Some poet in his by-gone trance
Hath penned his rhyme to man
And drunk from out God's loving cup
And drawn those words that ran.
But whence come true man's radiant lore
By way to rainbow's end??
Tis is but an illusive rhyme
A sonnet tossed to the wind!

As humans gaze up to God's skies
And visualize the man
Who bore those ravages from out this earth
Time and time again
Those radiant beams from setting sun
Hath give us all God's gold
Right here in nature's glorious works
God's rhyme hath scarce been told!

The potter in all his labors
Can mold a vessel true
The one that holds the dewdrops
And quences man's thirst anew
For we in all our ponderance
Can bide some time alone
And drink from out God's blessings
Until our rhyme hath song!

The starry heavens so awesome
Those millions of comet trails
And heaven with all its wonders
And the horrendous, scornful hell
All are but for the asking
God's roads from time born old
Whence cometh the weary traveler
To choose his eternal goal!!!

OUR FINEST HOURS

In time there'll come a sacred pause
After work tis put out of way
Where no man drinks the vineyard's wine
And no evil mars Earth's day.
There truly shall fashion a tranquil stance
Where God and man join power,
Where love and respect hold high esteem
For this tis our finest hour!

After the chore is put to rest,
After the clock strikes eight,
There'll come a hush from Ole Uncle Ben
As the Biblical text tis spake.
We learn of Paul, Peter, and Luke
And yearn for that higher power
Where God and kingdom and man join hands
For this tis our finest hour!

The prodigal son, God's children that play
Along life's precarious path,
And the Pharoah king that pushed his way
And Moses striking his staff.
For these are not the intangibles to hold
For Earth twasn't meant to sour,
Love so sincere and respect for all
These in our finest hour!

The lark flies high o'r hills and dales,
The robin sings heaven's sweet tune,
And love longs melodize some lonely heart
While lilies bloom in the June.
For when God's nature manifests the day
And when Earth's beauty has power
Ah, grateful to the things of joy,
These in our finest hour!

In time we'll learn of the right and the wrong,
In life we'll witness many a kill
Of sacred sheep that went to slaughter
And blood and Earth's tears spill.
But that shouldn't stop us from turning the minute
Into some memento higher;
For poems and verse and peace with our God,
This is our finest hour!

The skies, so blue, do awe the eye
From Earth's fragile crust to space
And willowbrooks flow through hill and the dale
And deer abide with a grace.
For freedom and beauty and God and the life
And times when the coin has no power,
These are the moments that were meant to last,
These are our finest hours!

WHAT THE FLAG MEANS TO ME

Alone in the night in some trying fight
as flames light up the sky,
There lie three colors of flowing truth—
Three colors I won't deny.
She's red, white, and blue old cloth
Some banner, I've been told,
That men will give their lives away
For freedom and her hold!

She's a'flowing in the Far West
Across the Montana sky.
She's a'blowing in old Kentucky
As young folks watch her fly.
How proudly she gives her courage
To the eyes that all may see.
She meant the most to my folks
And she means the most to me.

There's a'calling in my starved soul
That longs for her gentle name,
And some soldier salutes her proudly
And guards her righteous fame.
She brought her peace and courage
To this nation in its test.
She'll do the same for you, friend,
She's an angel at her best!

There are mountains and gentle valleys
She guards in her great reign,
And some drifter in our city
Cries when he hears her name.
There are school kids and old folks
That proudly wave her on—
She's a martyr to freedom's glory,
How proudly we sing her song!

She's a'flowing over the fishers
In Florida's Tampa Bay.
She's a'blowing over Kansas
As farmers stack their hay.
How proudly she gives her courage
To the eyes that all may see.
She meant the most to my folks
And she means the most to me.

I hear some rushing trauma
Lies in her well-worn path,
And some country out to get her
And inflict its culture's wrath.
But don't you one minute worry,
The old girl will come on through.
She's guarding our hard-fought glory
Just like she wants to do!

She's a'flowing in Nebraska
As farmers shuck their corn.
She's a'blowing over Mississippi
As truck drivers toot their horns.
How proudly she gives her courage
To the eyes that all may see.
She meant the most to my folks
And she means the most to me.

As I humbly end my flag song,
I think of those in the cold.
Those slaves to starving nations
Who are killed while seeking goals.
And I thank my God in His glory
For saving this flag for me,
As I write this last verse of poetry
Down on my trembling knee!

She's a'flowing on a moonbeam
Up high in God's own turf.
She's a'blowing o'er this spaceball
That some call planet earth.
She's a'flowing over all free men
And those who long to be free
Just right there beside Ole Glory
That's what she means to me!!!

————————————

AMERICA FOR ALL
(A Song)

As the world events rob the world
And kingdoms rise and fall
As endless lines of armies fight
And rulers claim their all,
there is a haven, a solace fair,
Men grasp and seek her fame.
There is America strong and proud
Before this world aflame!

Oh, America, great America,
Our boundless, endless land
Please take the charge the world hath thrown
And right the race of man.
Comfort all who seek your soil
And pave that golden way
Into this land where freedom lives
And shelter all who stray!

Kingdoms rise and kingdoms fall
And mankind yearns for peace
And scholars with their able minds
Predict a war-like trek.
But there is strength beyond this hour
That is strong and fair
America, our great America,
With glory in the air!

Oh, America, America,
We call upon your name
Lead us into tranquil times
Far from this world aflame.
Comfort all who long for peace
And guard God's righteous name
This land of brimming, freedom's pride
America! Right proclaimed!

Years pass on and times do change
And children go to play
And old folk with their aging charms
love the American way.
For lives are strong and pride doth show
By all who claim her soil
America, our great America,
Forever! Strong and loyal!

Oh, America, America,
The world yearns for your flame.
The strength from out your beaming land
God strong with righteous fame.
Many who crave thy glories true
And all who seek her sod
Proclaim this land where freedom lives
'Tis heaven made by God!

As poets draw their thoughts to ink
And nights are dark and cold
As stars shine high above this land
There is a sacred goal.
It is the noble challenge took
Our land so proud and free.
There is America one and all
For all the world to see!

Oh, America, our America,
With glory in her land
With workers on her shipyards
To farmers toil in hand
From cities high with towers
To country courthouse squares
America! Our great America!
Is everyone's to share!

AMERICA'S SONG OF TRIUMPH
(Thank God for Liberty)

Through the fiery night we fought
With flares that lit the sky.
We sent our missiles on their way
Saying, "liberty or die."
Our gallant, streaming banner flows
Under God's protected wings.
Oh, Christ, our Great Redeemer,
Our God, Our Saving King!

Oh, land; oh, soil, our forefathers tilled—
let us win this fire fight now,
Please let us do Your will.
Keep our country the hope she is
And keep our children free.
Let us love thy freedom shores
Thank God for liberty!

The land was aglow as gallant men
Turned a sacred page
And the sky was lined with crimson red
As soldiers fought the rage.
Each bleeding soul that passed that night
Died not in vain nor shame.
They died to keep our liberty
So God could write their names!

A poet fool, such as I,
Can pen this verse by night,
While gallant soldiers fight to keep
Our freedoms and our rights.
The freedoms that we live each day
T'was not bought with pen.
They were bought with tears and blood
From decent, honorable men!

I hear the cannons burst at night,
I know the skies are full
Of men who bravely fly the land
Where Washington and Lincoln stood.
For men who give their quenching breaths
So fools, as I, are free,
I rhyme this poem to them all
Wherever their souls might be!

Oh, land; oh, soil,
That our forefathers tilled.
Lord, let us win this fire fight now,
Please let us do your will.
Keep our country the hope she is
And keep our nation free.
Let us love thy freedom shores
Thank God for liberty!

———————————

LIFE'S CHALLENGE

Through strife and pain and heartbreak
We Christians hold our faith
And witness to the sinners
And try to show God's grace.
For Christ our saving master
Hath given each so free
Salvation for our needing
And heaven endlessly.

Oh, Jesus Lord of mercy,
Thou hath given your life
Upon Golgotha's hilltop
By storm and fury's might.
For thou hath paid the price
For each of us in need
And drawn our special treasures
Towards heaven's endless seas.

As life holds our measures
Of pleasures that we lay
And draw our every beings
Upon eternal ways
We, each, shall look to Jesus
The one who sets us free
Our Lord, our God, our Master,
Loves all so endlessly.

From time's own grand beginning
God's stars hath seen the faith
Of Christ's eternal forever
And never-ending grace.
For little do we earthlings
Live our lives as planned
We falter by the wayside
And flounder in time's sand.

God's heavens hold those treasures
Where shall abide the ones
Christians who gave their hearts
To Jesus Christ the son.
And in our earthly rhythms
We, too, can share so free
Our witness and confessions
And living our lives for He.

As time 'tis long and painful
We Christians hold our faith
For Jesus, Lord and Master
Has given strength so great.
And in our ever longings
We all shall strive for him
And show our earthly brothers
The need to let Him in.

LIFE'S ENCORE AND FINALE

We are all like grains of sand
Sifting through some hourglass
Moving, hence, through walls of time
Drawing on our somber past.

From morn to dark and in between
We plan and plot our mode
And cast our song to our the wind
And garner what cleans our soul.

From out our dark and surging ways
And by God's book we swear our hearts
And hurl to sea our sinking ships
Not knowing, whence, we shall embark.

Our toils and deeds in follies share
Our chores to which we shan't hath done
For by our lives we each hath spoken
Our tongues shall be our death and run.

As scars upon our lagging flesh
And tears from out our saddened eyes,
We each hath drawn our measures spent
For God will hold us to our lies.

From out this life of sobs and tears
From out time in labored lay,
We each hath found eternal crowns
And bid our years forever's way!!!

———————

GONE FOREVER

The works we humans sow and seed
Are but the wind's own rustling thrust,
Blowing forever across our tracks
Erasing all our paths and ruts.

Upon the coming amplitude
That zenith of our lives portrayed,
Our tears and fears throughout our years
Shall fade and vanish from their rage.

As looming o'er our wants and cares
'Tis father time in all his score
Casting each our faiths and deeds
Upon time's wretched evermore.

And, too, we men in tearful quest
Who toiled and slaved throughout our best
We shall vanish from the page
Of eternal, endless, awesome jest.

As pillows of some kingdom's hall
Which hold our hearts above the flood
They shall surely crumble within
And drown our hearts in our blood.

From out this world that holds our lays
And by the shores of time's own sea
We each shall board that ship of faith
And sail throughout what we chose free!

———————

REFLECTIVE POET

Upon the coming imminent quest
By eternity's intransitive night
The poet spills his vagrant tears
Of loves and fears and sights.

This world he chose in brazen thought
Hath gained not ounce of him
The poet alludes not only self
But all this earth of men.

From out time's starry foreverness
Comes forth the call of rhyme
'Tis not this fool in sacredness
But all his thoughts entwined.

The rapture, hence, 'tis stark and brief
And rhythm hath no end,
Only those of lucid self
Shall word right to the end.

The forever, endless, blissful mess
'Tis glorified his words
Of seas and ale and thoughts prevailed
And visualized his verbs.

A child born to the great divide
Of land and rolling sea
The poet hath but run his race
And rhymed both you and me

As time moves on to endless sky
And God doth come for me
The wretched, hard, eternal run
Holds all the fool of me!

DAWN OF TIME

From out the fiery, molden mass
With boiling fury all entwined
Upon some blackened, starless night
With ebony depths of eternal kinds,
Our God hath moved his prophetic hand
And hurled his mighty awesome charge
And flung the molden, eternal heat
To born creation and all his stars!

Upon the swirling, forever sight
Beyond a human's frail-like stance
God hath sent his starry night
To time and place with all enhanced.
With suns and moons and lands untold
God hath swayed infectious might
And borne his love throughout his fold
Creation! the dawn's first light!

With infinite depths no one can stare
And distance beyond the grasp of man,
God hath brought his promised signs
Before his own with sea and land.
For God hath placed into his dawn
Life! From out his universe large
And borne his beings upon those earths
Throughout his eternal brilliant stars!

Throughout the cooling, ever mix
Intransitive with His angel bands
God hath casts His starry sea
Before the eyes and souls of man
And drawn His will with love and peace
And placed before his awesome sight
Glory! In the highest esteem
And moved this earth with morning's light!

The breathing flesh God made in kind
And eyes to gaze up to his stars
And pulse and wealth beyond our words
Hath shown us humans
"How great God art."
And through this darkened abyss depths
All placed throughout God's eternal void
Are moved the very years we played
Upon this land made by our Lord!

The flowing currents by stars and seas
And thrust upon the milky way
'Tis creation's dawn enhanced by love
And comet's trails that streak away.
From out the ever endless sight
All hung in glory's rapturous love
Are jewels that twinkle upon some night
And God and Christ and angels above!

The pulse of time hath drawn its wealth
From out God's generous, gracious hand
And brought its living life in time
Riches from some foreign land.
For flickering lights throughout God's void
And years and tears upon our rues
All comprise our berth in rhyme
And paid us what t'was rightly due!

The matter that t'was spread around
And sands of time in glorious rhyme
T'was granted God's own rightful stance
Upon this stage of life and kind.
For all God's heart strings hold ourselves
Into His soothing, loving grace
And all our treasures hold the keys
To future tense and eternal faith!

Through depths and highs and plain between
across God's wondrous milky way
'Tis life throughout time's starry sea
Which God hath drawn in perfect stay
And end on end his ever role
Doth move our hearts to infatuately say,
"What hath we done for out his Son
Shall place our souls in eternal lay!"

The birth of all 'tis by some creed
Which God Almighty hath seeded hence
And creation before our very hearts
Doth show God's own right, intent.
For all the stars and all the seas
And all in all our very souls
Shall find their place throughout the void
Forever! In His endless role!!!

———————————

STARWARD DESTINY

The wind and sky and great beyond
Shall carry me home tonight
And pull my very soul along
Time's moving, endless flight.

The systems old in grand display
And stars throughout God's sea
Shall ferry my every thoughts I bore
And find eternity.

Those deeds and tools I laid to rest
And all my very words
Shall falter upon God's imminent score
And fade throughout this world.

For bands of angels with beautiful robes
And God's harmonious ways
Shall draw my heart from which it bore
My rhymes and disarrays.

Those stars upon God's forever night
And life from out the void
All hold my faith and destiny
And pull me to my Lord.
For God hath placed upon my grave
A song—"He is not there"—
And moved His mighty hand along
My path to heaven's care.

forever in some perfect tune
The sky shall come for me
And place my rhymes all along since gone
In heaven endlessly!

———————

PEACE WITH JESUS

Throughout the eternal heavens
Our God hath shown his hand
And brought our very beings
Into his generous plan
And given to each his children
Jesus who paid the price
For God hath loved us humans
And He hath graces our lives.

Jesus, Lord of Mercy,
Bring us to our knees
Make we humble humans
Love you and believe.
Draw us to the Father
And save us in our days
Give each child who asks for
Heaven by the way.

As days turn into sorrow
And years turn into scars
Draw us to your presence
And place us by your stars.
Steer our way to glory
With blood from out the lamb
And greet each striving Christian
With thou outstretching hands.

Oh, Lord, our greatest Master,
Who made the mighty sea
Of stars and moons and planets
Give us the eyes to see
Thou forever beautiful heaven
Beyond time's distant shore
And place our every measure
Into thee evermore.

Our skin doth age with wrinkles
And tired we move our hearts
And cast our thoughts towards heaven
We know "how great Thou art."
For us in all our wonderings
Hath come from out to see
Jesus Christ our Savior
Who loves us endlessly.

We stand before our Master
And we shall hear our names
For God hath opened henceforth
His book of eternal reigns
For great our perfect Master
Hath placed our hearts to rest
And sent us on to glory
With Jesus and all His best.

———————————

GOD'S PLAN

From out this life of troubled times
And by the treacherous paths we walk
Our God hath given guiding hand
And steered us toward those things He wrought.
For each and every soul we bring
Unto God's eternal, saving faith
Shall pay our pass unto His stars
And place us by His blessed grace.

Our Lord, our God, from out the shores
Of his moving, grandest sea
Thou art mighty before our lives
Thou art peace so plain to see.
We worship God in all our ways
And strive for peace before our part
We live each day by gracious faith
And know that God hath us at heart.

The morning sun hath cast its light
Upon God's mighty loving plan
And moved our eyes and hearts delight
To Jesus with his outstretched hands
We long to wash our Master's feet
And place before his path to see
Our hearts with loving thoughts to share
And praise our Master endlessly.

Jesus is the prince of peace
And God 'tis at the master helm
For children, each, we one and all
Long for love to come right in.
Along our weary paths we plod
And through this life of struggling ways
We pause and see God's beautiful world
And all His gracious, saving ways.

The role we take in this old world
'Tis but a fleeting, flickering flame
For there 'tis grander, starlight lore
Unto God's forever, eternal reign.
Our chores and works will one day cease
And Jesus shall in all His might
Come for those who hold his faith
And those for whom hath loved his life.

Our lives are born from in this world
And heaven reigns from out the sky
For Jesus Christ in all His fame
Hath paid the price for you and I.
And one day, hence, shall forth be heard
God's triumphs in a grand display
For each and every one of us
Shall find eternal, forever way!

———————————

FOREVER AND FOREVER

Forever and forever
God's tide comes rolling in
And pounds the balmy seashore
And pulls the souls of men.
For eternal as the endless sky
Above the cares of man
God's timeless, endless sea of stars
'Tis all creation's plan!

Forever and forever
We scholars word our fears
And garner up what pays our way
Into this world of tears.
For each small rhyme we pen by heart
'Tis all some trivial spree.
Our words shall fade through minutes past
And die from out our glee!

Forever and forever
God's verse 'tis grand and true
From out His glory upon His stars
Our deeds are all past due.
For each and every verse we pen
through devious and embroiled
Our tongues shall spill our utterances fair
And slave our hearts to toil!

Forever and forever
Jesus is the only way
To stand out from the crowd
For venomous pursuits with coin invest
Hath drawn their own deed
And salvaged all what armies left
And drown them in our need!

Forever and forever
The poet pours his soul
Upon some lonely seabrook
With currents swift and cold,
And casts his pen upon the page
And bleeds his heart to tears
And waits for out the Master's call
To take us to our peers!

Forever and forever
As armies bide their way
Into some tranquil village fair
And pilfer all the way.
God's lasting, eternal, forever rhyme
Shall then pluck each lost man
And hurl them into darkness where
The evils draw their clan!

Forever and forever
God's sky stands as His dream
Upon the suns and planets far
From creation's dawn and scene.
His wondrous glory holds our hearts
Of each of us who share
And paves our passage upon His stars
To heaven! With our cares!

Forever and forever
God's timeless, endless Son
Hath all exalted glories fair
And paid the price and won.
And, we, who hold His sacred tunes
Shall one day find our home
Into His vast, moving sea
Forever! In His song!

ETERNAL ALL

From out the starry, infinite space
From dawn of creation's light
Through billions of years of starbeams bent
We gaze God's Holy might.
For God hath moved His mighty hand
And seeded us on this earth
And granted souls our earthly roles
And gave us eternal worth!

The cock crows once from out our scene
the beautiful sun has risen
For God hath stirred His cleansing breeze
And granted the ocean rhythm
Those mighty peaks which share God's sky
Are laden with snow away,
For all 'tis rightful, blessful myrrh
they are for our stay!

The teeming woods with life abound
The valleys lush and green
And fields of clover with daisies fair
Are all God's beautiful scene.
For we who share earth's wonderful worth
Hath all our lives invest
To draw upon God's giving hand
And reap its eternal best!

The skies are full of soaring fowl
And the wind 'tis on our face
For God hath stirred His mighty breeze
And given life to taste.
For out God's love 'tis all so free
He stands so true and loyal
And all we humans are meant to be
His own and granted toilers.

The ocean's depths are deep and dark
With life that holds our awe
And beaches white with lapping waves
Hath all our thoughts to draw.
For we in our frailty share
God's timeless, endless sea
That great, eternal, forever worth
That sets our souls to free!

The deserts lure of rough terrain
And gorges steep and wide
And streams that wash the soul of earth
Hath God's amazing pride.
For out His worth He admonished us
We humans in worldly trance
To roam throughout His sacred land
And bide our earthly stance!

As we in all our wailing ways
Are caught up in our flings,
We humans trek throughout our lives
To catch the wealth of things.
We ponder whence our next of sales
Shall pay our way to roam
And never once amid God's worth
Stop to see our wrong!

As I must end this morning's verse
And pull my life to work,
Throughout God's beautiful, wonderful day
All filled to brim with worth,
I stare upon His eternal land
That God hath given free
And thank my lucky stars above
For all God's love to me!

EARTH'S CHANGING FACE

This land 'tis free and all t'was said
God's world shall be some day,
For wrong cannot endure so long
Evil will fall by the way.

This old Earth will be free, you see,
And men shall start anew;
Those tiring slaves that till the soil
Will reap a harvest true.

And as these prophetic words slip past
Those decades sown with strife,
The wonders that shall come from God
Console us through the night.

This poet fool in all his blunders
Shall bow before his King,
As church bells ring throughout this land
And angels shout and sing.

The walls of each forbidden city
Each Jericho one and all
Shall fall down flat before the sound
As Christ ascends His throne.

The blasphemous turf where devils roam
Shall dissolve before God's light,
And only Christ and love and peace
Will displace Earth's darkest night.

The weak and meek, the widower and beggar
Shall rise before their peers
As droves of angels herald in
And dry their shedding tears.

Each fool that hoarded his cherished coin
And wicked and evil men
Shall beg the hallowed Son of God
To pardon their omnibus sins.

But, nay, not shall the sword be spared
The book of life shall read
Each pagan in his waxful worth
Shall fall and death impede.

The hungry child with starry eyes
The sick and trampled souls
Each Lazarus from his humble cot
Shall reap their long-sought goals.

As kingdoms fall and blades are bent
And fashioned into plows,
Some poet in his faltering verse
Shall expound "God's time is now."

The oceans in their age-old lash
Each wave from time's own song
Shall spew the past soul they hold
And right each wreck long gone.

As dawn breaks o'er this staggering hand
And ink flows from the page,
What talent gave this poor word slave
Shall never leave the grave.

As night draws forth its melodious sounds
And each page has portrayed
Shall silence before God's hour hand
And reap what it has saved.

This Earth will be in latter days
And those beneath the stone
Shall rise and take the hand of Him
As heaven calls home its own.

For this Earth will meet those prophetical signs
And draw from its new life
From out that endless, boundless realm
Of God and glory's might.

All space and time and stars and moon
Shall one day hence be gone,
For God hath given the blood of Christ
To call man's soul to home!

————————————

FOREVER

From out the eternal, forever space
We humans share in time
Through eons wrought with loving care
There comes a sacred rhyme.
God's burning zeal of loving care
Hath all been charged to me
To share His eternal, lasting love
And live our lives to be!

Through dark and uncertain miles we plod
Along this endless road
From creation's dawn to glory's place
We hath been in God's role
To live throughout our fleeting lives
And show our hearts each one
God's greatest work upon this place
Jesus! Who hath won!

God's infinite mist of fiery space
Doth cover earth's chilling nights
And systems born old from light years spent
Hath all our tears to write.
Upon God's generous, loving heart
We each hath drawn our wage
And paid the endless, timeless night
Our charity and rage!

From eternal dawn to present tense
God hath evoked His say
Through Biblical lore and loving works
He gave His heart away.
And deeded each us human frail
His Son to set us free
Upon His starry brilliant night
To save our souls to be!

The dawn of time hath seen it all
From each self-righteous man
Mutiny by the hoard of crowds
And death upon God's plan.
For each and every lot we cast
Hath drawn our hearts to be
Worldly lords of pitiful prose
Who evoke the devil's spree!

As moving hands doth write our wage
And stardust hath flowed free
We place our eternal, forever berth
In time's endless sea.
And gather up what wares we claim
Our own and rightful spoils
And draw our gold from out time's bank
And chart our souls to toil!

As we must end this living space
And go to join the sky
That eternal, ever, endless surf
That pulls our souls to fly
We, in meager, senseless tasks
Shall all land each one see
That grant, conclusive time we bore
Drained of all our glee!

We hath been charged within our souls
Upon this land of tears
Where armies wrought with devil's lust
To right our hearts sincere.
For each and every move we place
Our eternal, forever berth
Into time's moving, endless space
For out God's timeless worth!

JESUS, LORD OF MERCY
(A Song)

There was a small, young child
Born unto this earth
Brought here by the Father
To give us saving worth.
And in our times of sorrow
We all can look to Him,
Jesus, Lord of Mercy,
Who saves us from our sin.

Oh, Jesus Christ, we love you
For us you gave your life
Saving grace for many
And comfort in our strife.
Oh, Lord, our God, our Master,
To you we cast our eyes
And look up to your heavens
And long to see you nigh.

In our every weakness
We humans grope our way
Throughout our lives of needing
And by our sorrow's way.
But, Jesus, you have brought us
Grace and peace so free
To save us from our sinning
And love us endlessly.

By day's own light we work toward
Our chores in labors lay
And strive to glimpse the morrow
And reason in our way.
But, Christ, our Lord, and Master
Hath given all to me
Salvation for earth's many
And eternity all so free.

As Jesus cares for many
He also loves each one,
Children of His earthland
Awaiting His return.
And in our darkest moments
We all can call on Him
To pull us from our sinning
And place us in His kin.

While men hath trying heartbreaks
And earth holds hate and lust
Our Lord, our God, our Master,
Hath given each His worth.
He loves us in our stumbling
And never will forsake
His children by His wayside
His love is free and great!

Oh, Jesus Christ, we love You
For us You gave Your life
Saving grace for many
And comfort in our strife.
Oh, Lord, our God, our Master,
To You we cast our eyes
And look up to Your heavens
And long to see You nigh.

———————————

TIME ETERNAL

As man stares at the firmament
God's space with stars untold,
He reasons by his instincts
That mighty is God's role.
And we His wayward children
Hath seen the works to be
Great God, Lord of creation,
And all the wealth so free.

Our God of all our Fathers
Thy will henceforth be done,
Thy grandest, beautiful love strokes
Hath brought this earth Your Son.
From out thy boundless power
Thy Christ hath set us free
And draws our longing heart throbs
To righteous, kinder He.

Intuned with glory highest
We Christians plod our way
From out this miring planet
Caught up in mortal's way.
And as we look around us
We see God's great own glee
His wondrous, eternal creation
For all our hearts to be.

By night into the darkness
Some thief comes forth to steal
And fetch our earthly treasures
And flee with pockets filled.
But he shan't pull our spiritual
Souls into his plan—
Only God hath power
O'er all and each of man.

The devil holds the sinner
Into his treacherous trance
And tries to seed iniquities
Unto men's hearts enhanced.
But, nay, he shan't forth prosper
He shall in time be shunned
Only God Almighty
Shall last from out the Son.

The winds of sky seem tranquil
The sun sets in the west
And God's own lovely moonbeams
Hold each our hearts at rest.
And fairer 'tis Christ's message
Unto the earth at large
Only time eternal
Shall last from out God's stars.

————————

CHRISTIAN'S SONG

The power to be a Christian
'Tis given by the Son.
Jesus Christ of Nazareth
Grants glory to each one
Of those who ask forgiveness
And those who pray to see
Heaven for eternity
And peace forever free.

Our Jesus, Lord Almighty
Thou peace forever reigns
Upon eternity's lasting
Forever endless name
And fairer 'tis Christ's kindness
Bestowed unto this land
A world of wondrous wonders
Wherein we take Christ's hand.

Led by a perfect promise
We Christians plod our way
Throughout this world a'turning
And by eternity's way.
Along the road to heaven
We stop and feel God's love
Wherein we passed forthwith
Throughout this earth in love.

Jesus Christ of Nazareth
Hath all the grace for me
Enough to fill time's oceans
Enough to make men free,
For if we closely listen
We shall hear those words,
Those songs God's wind doth whisper
To all they shall be heard.

Drawn up in time's deceiving
Tearful, selfish ways
We children of the Master
Hold close to Christ today.
We walk and talk with Jesus
And henceforth shall abide
Into a life of meaning
And walk close by Christ's side.

As years turn into decades
And times pass fleeting on,
We look and gaze the starlight
And press close on to home.
For Jesus shall forth cometh
One day for each to see
And pull our very heart strings
And place us close to Thee.

———————————

JESUS, JESUS, JESUS

Oh, Jesus, Jesus, Jesus,
We love Your wonderful name
Your saving grace hath paved the way
To heaven where You reign.
Your beautiful love hath made our hearts
A tranquil, eternal part
Of heaven with its streets of gold
By whence eternity starts.

Oh, Jesus, blessed Jesus,
We long to hold your hand
And wash Your feet and worship You
Throughout the years at hand.
We honor You and talk to You
With all our humble hearts.
We know from our Christian lives
How great You truly art!

Oh, Jesus, Jesus, Jesus,
We call upon thy name
The prince of peace of eternity
How great 'tis is your fame.
We bow before your mighty stance
By time's eternal shore
And cast our eyes upon the sea
Of stars forevermore.

Oh, Jesus, Jesus, Jesus,
We dream of Thee sublime,
Thy great and powerful Lord of all
Who gave us wealth in kind.
Thy presence hath but moved our way
And made a part of me
Our souls hath found our tranquil home
In heaven endlessly!

Oh, Jesus, Jesus, Jesus,
Earth's days can be so dark
And evil lurks beyond our doors
And death holds each its part.
But in our hours of living
We see Thy wondrous plan
And make our way to Thee to stay
Throughout all time at hand!

Oh, Jesus, Jesus, Jesus,
We see your love and cry
And know within our spiritual hearts
That we shall never die.
We long for You and come to You
For our eternal rest
And sing your songs with earth all gone
And love your righteousness!

————————

JESUS CALLS

As Jesus calls for sinners
He also loves each child
Children of his earthtown
Where each of us abide.
He speaks so soft and gently
And draws us to Himself.
With arms wide open stretching
He gives us spiritual wealth.

Oh, Jesus Christ, our Master,
Who rules upon his throne,
Forever and forever
He loves us by his songs.
Through choruses of angels
He brings us hymns to sing
And opens up our blessings
For all who praise our king.

While flowers grow in meadows,
And robins sing in tune,
Our greatest, grand own master
Hath blessed this day in bloom.
And sprinkled grace around us
So love shall make our day
Upon his beautiful hilltop
Throughout his world today.

The great love God gives us
Can bring man to his king.
With God's own special message
A soul can spiritually sing
And pave the way to heaven
For those once lost in pain
Christ even gave us blessings
For all who call His name.

As Jesus calls for mercy
Before His Father's court,
He speaks so plain and gently
For all who made the port
And as our ship of sailing
Draws nigh unto his sea
Our souls hath found their harbor
In heaven endlessly.

The world hath held the teardrops
Of sinners in their day
Of men who felt the follies
Of death along life's way.
But there is grander glory
For all who call Christ's name,
Their souls shall fly to heaven
And eternally ever reign!

———————

FREEDOM'S SONG

As sun doth lift its beaming rays
Upon God's grandest throne
He made our land as He had planned
And gave us miles to roam.
We each are His great work of art
For God hath made the soil,
This land where freedom lives and thrives
Through our work and toil.

Oh, America, America,
Our own great land of home
We speak of your own boundless love
Your grand skies and your songs.
We each shall find our long-sought dream
And in time we hath stood
Before God's greatest freedom's home
Throughout this land so good!

As time doth slip away with years
And our hearts long for youth
As days do pass as fading dreams
Our God holds them in truths.
We think of all His glorious land
America! For our home!
And all those freedoms beneath His stars
To guide us as we roam.

Oh, America, America,
Your land 'tis what we deemed
A haven for some longing hearts
A mecca for a king.
As time doth bide our granted stance
Upon this land of home,
We all shall say she's good as gold
And claim her for our own!

Through years and tears of passing times
When we were young and keen,
Our rightly thoughts of God's great land
Shall see us to our King.
And as we stand before God's all
His land of freedom's bars
Our hearts shall find their solace there
With Jesus and His stars!

Oh, America, America,
This land of young and old
This haven for some longing hearts
This land of God's own fold.
Our eyes doth lift beyond the hour
And go to meet God fair
And thank Him for this grateful gift
Our land! He made with care!

As we must end our freedom's song
And as we go our ways,
We each hath taken something good
Of wonders God hath made.
It 'tis this love throughout His land
This land God made so free
And called upon His mighty Son
To love us endlessly!

Oh, America, America,
Our hearts doth move with awe
As we reflect the heart of Him
Who died to save us all.
For we shall truly always love
God's greatest freedom's land
This country that Christ paid the way
To take us in His hand.

CREATION

Born of love and endless grace
Through flaming firmament so wide
By time's eternal, awesome bliss
Our God hath sanctified
And given His stars their brilliant hues
Upon eternity's endless range
From out His matter shaped so true
To glorify His mighty reign!

As sparkling upon the firmament's way
So awesome as God's magnificent strokes
The colors of His greatest act
T'was love abound He carefully wrote.
By way of joy He granted skies
To each and own He set in place
His grand array of lovely notes
To sooth the soul and give us grace!

The milky mist of billions of lights
Confront the eye to see
All time eternal from end to end
Stretching above the beautiful sea.
The endless clouds so full of bloom
Serenade the fowls which fly so high
From lasting works to loving souls
God made the poet, prophet, and I!

The eternal night which grips the soul
And billions of jewels upon the deep
And mortal man with mundane ways
Bequeath the poet a rhyming trek.
To put to words God's greatest acts
Tis sheer folly by human ways
We bide our time of rhythmic stance
And reap what we have cast away!

This terrestrial world with all its strife
And kingdoms wrought with evil men
And frivolous greeds that tempt us all
Has God Almighty saddened within
For time doth move to some new page
And scribe eternal our worldly jest
To come back right to haunt us all
Before the great foreverness!

Before we toil from night to day
And loose within our grip and hold
Upon this bountiful, wondrous earth
To free our hearts and our poor souls.
We cast our eyes upon earth's plain
And gaze above an awesome sight
Great God Almighty residing where
The angels hung His starlit night!

Time's moving ink afronts our works
From dust to dawn we poets write
And spell whatin doth draw our souls
Upon our Makers' loving sight.
For peace is what He hath us do
In our meek rhymes we earn our way
To journey from this turbulent land
And meet with Him so far away!

The boiling sun ten thousandfold
With fires that flair and warm our earth
Where only Him, the Greatest One,
Can move about His endless berth.
And deep upon His void in view
A loving, euphoric, warming lay
'Tis cast upon some poet's page
And rhymes doth draw his words to say!

A billion, billion specks of light
And Gabriel's journey throughout God's void
And many songs sung this night
Move within our sacred Lord.
For He hath made the ocean's vest
To cover land and bring new life
And draw from out His bountiless rhymes
To move some soul to saving light!

The tallest pinnacle cuts the sky
The burning sun doth start our day
And bathes God's world with warmth and love
As man, with words, rhymes away.
For as some lark, above this land
Soars with endless, soothing flight
God's vast, eternal, loving best
'Tis what gives us our inward sight!

Those rays from out some distant star
Which travel eternally from time's own end
Hath scarce to reach this minute rock
We call our earth, entrenched with sin.
Alone held firm by God's own hand
The infinite depth we shan't perceive
Earth's little man hath weeped and wept
Upon time's own right disbelief!

As endless as God's moving tide
Which fronts some island in His sky
And cleanses vagrant, diminished shore
With love and life and never dies.
It draws our souls His great quest
His wondrous space we call our home
And gives the poet his rhyming best
And says that we are not alone!

The greatest river's current flow
Which moves over rocks and gives the stream
Its cleansing, rightful, vibrant best
Confronts the eye that hath so seen.
It washes all in its own way
And draws new life from out its quest
And gives each tongue its quenching thirst
To sustain our souls in foreverness!

As nights engulfed with war and strife
Spread across man's pitiful role
They dark his acts and worldly deeds
To hide so seemingly his goals.
And kingdoms wrought with wealth and quest
Confront our eyes in disbelief.
What hath man done with his great gift?
This earth and all its spiritual needs?

The teaming heavens alive with rhyme
Those brilliant hues of God's great act
And allusive space we shan't once hold
Hath scarce to give us what we lack.
Before our Maker we pitifully stand
Indulged with envy for some gold
We totter within our weak meek hearts
And pass God's wondrous, long-sought goals.

A penance with which to pay our way
Unto the height of glorious stance
Robs our souls betrayed by all
And fools our inklings like a trance.
We think that we the gifted ones
Can pull the death from out our hearts
And find our own eternal best
How fooled we are in callous starts!

The laborers' work 'tis never done
For only God can rest in time
And give each one his talents true
To glorify His wondrous signs.
For as we look at loving worth
And pull within our saddened hearts
We see the Great Jehovah One
Who made us all in piece and part!

How many acts of truancy deeds
We humans commit throughout our stay
Upon this rock we call our home
God knows it all by our weak lays.
And as He sees His grand own plan
Robbed of love with blasphemous turf
And foolish poets from out his rhyme
He saddens within his generous worth!

The sky hath draped it blue around
This starving earth for love and deed
And charitable acts from out the heart
Are what our God doth right believe.
He gives us strength along life's way
And draws His healing power's true
Upon this emaciated earth in time
And sanctifies His chosen few!

The fury of earth's storm is strong
And thunder rolls along unto
Some needing soul that is forlorn
And craving love and saving, too.
For as the glowing rhyme is penned
From out God's hand ensuing love
He who calls for heavenly bread
Shall reap it all from up above!

William Furr

As scholars plot and plan their way
Unto this learned earth so blind
And thinkers jest what come what may
And writers labor through their time.
They all should lean outside their berths
And stare and gaze into God's sky
And drop down on their knees and say
"Pluck the thorns from out our eyes!"

The years move swift from out the flesh
And mountains crumble wherein they stand
And graveyards haunt the aging hearts
For death will come with bony hands.
But all the mortal man can do
Is believe and love God's wondrous rhymes
And call upon His Great, Great Son
To give them peace within their time!

The laws of all t'wer written hence
By God Almighty in His scroll
And time eternal in present tense
Doth find our hearts in vagrant cold.
For as this world doth move to day
And dawn right shows God's wondrous hand
We foolish men upon this earth
Reject the one who made us man!

The beauty of the deep, dark forest
And lilies floating in seemingly trance
Upon some pond with tranquil promise
Reflects the love of nature's stance.
And fields of clover and laden hay
Along the paths we earthlings took
Show great the one who gave us all
Into His eternal saving book!

As we in all our waning ways
Reflect the signs of daily life
And busy as we poets seem
Are scarce to grasp God's infinite light.
We live by day and rest by night
And team throughout this wondrous land
For we, the chosen, rightful ones,
T'wer made by God's own blessful hand!

Time 'tis an allusive thought to grasp
And billions of lives are set in place
Upon this world with stars above
Along God's amazing Milky Way.
And trillions throughout the deep dark void
All life from born of endless age
Shows love from birth to aging worth
All things our Lord hath beautifully made!

As dark as Golgotha's Hill of Skull
Upon that stormy wretched place
Where Christ the Chosen Begotten Son
Died to give amazing grace.
And all the centuries come and gone
From out this turbulent, restless world
We humans hath scarce to see the rhyme
Given by Him in eternal love!

As Moses led his Israel true
From out the waters spaced and wide
Which part with God's own loving hand
And moved by Him forth right aside.
The thought that some great work t'was sent
'Tis more than many of us shall grasp
For each and every one called man
Must see the physical, proven past!

As cities besieged by armies strong
As Jericho in its greatest hour
Built walls on top of walls and then
Fight off some mongrel's conqueror's power.
The works we humans toil and make
Are but an allusive, temporal fling
Those walls we put between ourselves
Shall never stand the onslaught's sting!

We human poets as this one
Can sing his rhymes bequeath along
For what if we doth give the world
An encore in our final song?
The only thing that shall forth last
'Tis God's almighty perpetual rhyme.
It never bends or waivers naught
But stands the test of relenting time!

As earth in all its creation fold
Doth turn amid God's endless stars
And the face of the deep is on our brows
For soon we shall forthright embark.
Our stance upon this world may seem
Some history's writ of passing lay
But only God the Greatest One
Shall last throughout the coming day!

We sing unto the heaven's bold
And raise our prayers up high along
To God, the Greatest, Lasting King
Somewhere within His sacred home.
We know He watches all his best
And brings His words to us to say
"What hath thy done for some poor soul
Hath done to Me alone today!"

The oceans roll along in time
And beaches gleam in purest white
As man and centuries old and new
Draw all their acts with which to write.
And give those annals of the times
Their prominent, prudent place to be
Upon God's eternal lasting shelf
To save our works for all to see!

We reason by our frail-like minds
That we are made in His great sight
By the generous Almighty's saving bliss
Which serenades this earth with light.
We pull ourselves up from the mire
And try to wash our shameful past.
We break the heart of our great God
Who gives us life for all who ask!

The skies are clear this time of year
And fowls soar in their nature's pride
And small creatures of woods and brook
Are where they should henceforth reside.
But man, oh, man, upon some moon
Forsook his rightful, peaceful stay
And ran to meet the infinite sky
And left his saving, gracious lay!

The centuries past hold deeds within
As poets pen their thoughts away
And man and beast and eternal feats
Converge upon the Milky Way.
Those stars upon God's infinite bliss
Are shining for our Greatest One
Who gave us bread and life abound
And paid us what we truly won!

The starlit heavens with allusive space
And endless lights from out God's past
And darkness on the face of the deep
With life and love and all that last.
'Tis in our Maker's greatest pride
All given in hallowed, eternal love
From out His bountiless infinite best
Bequeathed to us from up above.

As I draw end to my meek rhyme
Which Lord of Ages hath moved my pen
From earth to heaven and in between
To love and life all spaced within.
We, in humble, rhythmic ways
Hath scarce to grasp His great, dark night
And move our thoughts away from earth
To His everlasting, redeeming sight!

The oceans roll along in rhyme
In the infinite sky with life invest
And billions and trillions of men like us
Alive from God's own lovingness.
Doth show His heavens above the earth
He made and gave from ages past
That all who bear the cross from Him
Will find their peace at longing last

The Hill of Skull some stormy night
And darkness on this pitiful earth
And God Almighty above our flights
Who draws His signs of eternal worth.
By these truths we hold works righteous
Shall last through time's infinite quest
And give to all who see His love
JESUS—AND ALL THE REST!

FINAL VOYAGE INTO THE INFINITE

Many a poet shall color the skies
In Earth's last voluminous stage,
From out of space and time and depth
As prophecies fulfill the age!

With hues, so bold, from script they stroked;
They'll rhyme man's perilous hours.
From cradle to grave to heaven knows where,
Billions await the hour!

That eternal thirst man hath for truth
Shall sustain him on his flight.
The proud, the meek, the starved, the fed
Will tremble at the Creator's might!

Whether one be rich beyond all dream
Whether he be lame or old
It makes not one ounce of difference
Earth's spirit shall relinquish its hold!

From awesome chasms man's mind hath scaled,
Through abysses stained with blood
Shall flow the eternal vacillating time
And silence the hawk and the dove!

Old folks at home, young babes in arms
And us caught in between
Shall rhyme into that infiniteness
And dissolve as snows of spring!

Boundless repertoires of thine earth
The zenith, the plain, and the pit
All will find not a stone behind
While heavens and darkness a'fix!

The trip into God's eternal void
Shall spiral with old nebulous man,
Whether Christian, Atheist, Arab, or Jew
Together, in unison, hand-in-hand!

The poets? Why they shall be busy
Coloring that exhuberating voyage,
With lyrics of love and glad tidings
Earth's star-train will leave in accord!

The colors now run all together;
They form a new land and new time.
That infinite rock called Earth
Hath elapsed into elusive rhyme!

God's fiery night alive with stars
Billions wait yet to be born;
Tho time and place and Earth, at large,
Have relinquished their discernable form.

———————

BE GRATEFUL

Tho th' dough ain't a'rising
An' a dog kills m'cat,
Tho th' mailman's a'missing
An' th' baby's diaper's wet,

Whether th' gods are angry
Whether some rain shall fall

I'm grateful fer m' blessings,
I'm grateful one an' all!

There's even a prankster a'calling
Wearing out m'phone,
An' some joker on th' streetcorner
Shaken his fist to th' bone.

Whether it's raining or it's snowing
Or whether it's time to give up,

I'm grateful fer m' blessings,
Every morning that I wake up!

My doctor bills are outrageous,
Lord, will they ever stop?
Th' banknote's long overdue
An' they're repossessing m' crop.

Whether it's stand in th' breadlines
Or whether it's time to give in

I'm grateful fer m' blessings,
Every time that I breathe in!

A war, I'm a'going to yonder
Boy, did I want to stay home;
They've even taken m' "Luckys"
Making we "roll my own."

Whether I fight in some fire fight
Or whether I drill instead

I'll be grateful fer m' blessings
Each time I go to bed!

The President stands a'high shoulder
O'er th' rest of us all,
An' th' national debt is a'staggering
I hope this ole country don't fall.

Whether I'm eating bologna
Or whether I don't eat a'tall

I'm grateful fer m' blessings
To be standing here at all!

Tho th' sun dims on th' shoreline
An' th' night chill grips me so,
I think about m' blessings
An' winter's oncoming snow.

Whether I make it or break it
Or whether I fare with th' tide

I'm grateful for all m' blessings
I'm grateful to be a'live!

———————

GOD'S WORD FOREVER

As millenniums of time and beams of light propagate from the birth of creation, God's endless, timeless universe shall always hold it in bosom and foster in its glory, his unshakable, word. As armies of kings and tyrannies drag themselves across some barren landscape and hurl death and destruction upon mortal man, there shall always manage to survive God's written holy text.

When the names of Lenin, Hitler, Stalin, and Mussolini are forever forgotten, and when giants such as Washington, Lincoln, and Jefferson are but forever erased from the pages of history, there will stand God's Holy Bible! And when meek writers, such as myself, are long forgotten, and when our bones are but dust and ashes upon God's world, there will somehow, somewhere, manage to endure God's Holy Word!

For mankind, in all his frailty of disposition, shall leave these voluminous chambers of learned scholars and effervesce upon the skies and seas of eternal creation! There, in all God's wondrous glory of the heavenly firmament, shall stand the word of God and His mission unto the heart and soul of mortal man!

As long as a human being shall draw his
breath of life and see what God
hath bestowed upon this earth, there shall
remain a sacred copy of the Holy Bible.
For as the centuries of this earth come and
go, and as empires of mankind as built
and then destroyed, there will always stand
the glory of God. His irresistible urge of the
Holy Spirit in someone's heart is
unforgettable, and the lure of Christ's
saving grace shall always remain true and
forever perfect...

MISSION ACCOMPLISHED

Through passing years in pensive rhyme
We each hath moved our hands
And drawn from out God's greatest time
Our work!—with sign at hand.
We garner up what man hath left
In vulnerable fleeting lays
And leave our beings upon Earth's soil
And go to eternal ways!

The hills we climbed upon this Earth
T'wer steep and rough it seems
And all those tears we shed throughout
Hath flowed the "sting" of things.
For our own judgements by their mark
Hath all evoked God's hand
And pressed His righteous, kind intent
Throughout what He hath planned!

The very scent of flowers fair
Intrigued our souls in bloom
For all hath left that failing Earth
To its own volatile tunes.
We each hath passed that trying hour
With all our hearts to blame
And stand in line before God's scroll
To wait for call of name!

As little precious memories hold
Our paths that we hath tread
We mark our place upon the sky
Where no man goes unfed.
There lies a better rhyme we knew
Far greater than time's fling
'Tis the Hallowed Son of Him
Who 'tis our Grandest King!

We lay our souls upon time's throne
And dry our tears away
For what we each hath left intact
Shall lure our friends to wage.
They each shall seek our spoils and wealth
What little left on Earth
And by God's pressing hour glass
Forgot we'd ever birthed!

As time grows long and deep and dark
Those roads we ran in vain
Hath all relinquished ruts we wore
And hold another's fame.
For as we leave this blasphemous Earth
The years turn into dust
And what we left hath little chance
Of lasting in its worth!

As this poor soul with pen in hand
Doth draw this rhyme by night
Our God, Great God, above us all
Hath planned our every write
And moved our rhythms by His way
To draw what we hath need
Our every provoked thought of verse
Implanted with His seed!

As time and stardust pass their way
Upon God's void at hand
And lightyears fly throughout some lore
With each our rhymes in hand
Those charitable notes we penned to Christ
Shall all exalt our Lord
And close His mission upon our time
Forever! In just accord!

AMERICA AND BEYOND

America and beyond
Across God's endless skies
Where no heart starves for freedom
Where liberty doth abide.
As we count each blessing
From out God's greatest worth
We find our sacred homeland
T'was blessed from out this Earth!

America and beyond
Which stretches far and wide
From street cars in the Far West
To Wall Street full of pride
From humble little children
To Presidents and their peers
We thank our Lord Almighty
For America through the years!

America and beyond
Away from kings and queens
Far from the Devil lurking
All safe and sound and keen
To thee we raise our voices
And praise what God hath made
This blessed, beautiful America
From out His wonderous age!

America and beyond
By poet's dimming lights
To night shifts of our laborers
To mornings' beautiful heights
From meadows green with clover
To rugged mountains' views
Our America, our wonderful America,
We love thy splendors true!

America and beyond
From out God's greatest test
Where soldiers stand so staunchly
To guard our loyal best
To hold our sacred freedoms
From harm throughout the days
And praise our greatest country
For all its wonderous ways!

America and beyond
From county's courthouse fair
To cities grand in splendor
To hilltops high in air
To weeping willows draping
Some beautiful lake in view
We find our blessed America
T'was made for me and you!

America and beyond
As lines on some man's page
Where we expound its wonders
And draw what God hath gauged
To put to word our nation
'Tis but a folly's myth
We shan't once hold its awesome
Love from out God's gift!

America and beyond
Across these endless skies
From out this teaming Earth
To heavens far and wide
We love our greatest country
Through years from out our age
And praise God's beautiful America
And exalt what "He" hath made!

PASSING OF THE TORCH

I pass the eternal torch
To you! Ah, longing man,
From out time's infinite lore
Through words and rhymes at hand
And, er, some voluminous writ
Shall include me in its run
I shall perceive the flame
And word my time all done!

I pass the ambivalent call
Impended with rhyme that soothes
To calm man's eternal fears
From out time's forever moves
For words cannot alone
Evoke some sensational rhyme
All our doubts and fears
Hath signed their tears in time!

I pass to you the quest
Of mortals in their lay
Of time and centuries past
From out some scholar's grave.
As sure as dawn shall break
Through God's own glorious skies,
I pass my invested lore
And relinquish all words and die!

I pass to you the flame
Er, some men smother its call
From our Earth's dimlit past
As kingdoms and countries fall
Into God's dusts of time
Some poet's sense of review
I give all mine to that
Which draws its breath anew!

As poet and Earth compete
To spill their choice of deeds
Upon time's infinite skies
And place their souls in need
Toward God, our Greatest God.
Drawing what they include
They shall burn their flames
To that which they hath used!

And upon that traumatic day
I pass my torch to you
And bid ye each—ado!

THE ETERNAL WAIT

Upon this sacred place called Earth
We, each, must stand ensuing line
And hold our hands far out and reach
God's lasting, fleeting, awesome rhyme
And sing its songs of past gone lays
We drew upon our failing kinds
For whence we tire from out our stand
We draw our words to God's own rhyme!

Upon this tearful, sorrowful home
With all its pitiful sting of slave
We, each, must clasp our hands in prayer
And grieve for all those gone to grave.
As we invoke our rues and deeds
Upon this ball of tearful rage,
We stand in God's own endless line
And draw our souls by what He gauged!

Upon this blasphemous Earth of sorts
We toil in pious, king-like form
And boast we shan't accept our faiths
And cast our eyes to man's accord.
But, lo, the time shall forth deny
Our papers to the world at large
And place those men of divers' faiths
Into a sea of tears and scars!

Upon this aging mass we hold
Beneath our feet in potter's clay
Tis God's own rightful, blissful art
He made from out His firmament's way.
And as we each doth walk its miles
From out our birth's to death's own grave
We seek some measure of God's love
To place upon our grieving page!

As time doth move throughout God's world
We slaves must wait and endless toil
To draw our deeds upon time's sands
As God erases what each we soiled
And sea and foam and tide at hand
Hath all but washed and cleansed away
And made our wait to eternal faith
One shorter, grieving, painful stay!

TO BE AN AVERAGE PERSON

Oh, to be but an average person
Through Earth's relentless rain
With all my steadfast composure
And know that I am sane—
With wisdom that the gods infused
And demeanor of some rhyme
Into this vagrant lyric slave
That whines, whines, whines!

Oh, to be but an average person
Every night upon this earth
To have all my friends around me
And not be a rhyming surf—
To muse by joke and laughter
And not have a whim nor care
And count all my Earthly blessings
As if I was walking on air!

Oh, to be but an average person
With love and merriment of song
To spue forth verses of blessings
And serenade some lass all alone—
To have all those bountiful riches
Which some men hath made by their songs
And scale Earth's highest grand mountain
And view all the world from my throne!

Oh, to be but an average person
By the glow of a television set
To see all the strangest of mysteries
And hog all the food on the shelf—
To drink all the beer and kool-aid
And not think twice about work
To play all those wildest fantasies
And know that the night has its worth!

Oh, to be an average person
And count all those days to retire
And buy me a set of some golf clubs
And join all the boys and the guys—
To putt through life's monumental glories
And sleep as some lovers still do
And greet each newborn weekend
And pour down the ale and the brew!

Oh, to be but an average person
Through winter with all its cold
To buy me the warmest of jackets
And my wife a new pair of hose—
To play with my youngest of children
And tell them that Santa is near
And listen to all their heart dreams
As Christmas comes closer each year!

Oh, to be but an average person
All snug and cuddled in bed
With all those dreams of good times
I had by the book that I read.
And love my warm-heated lassie
Till earth and the morn bring anew
God's days in some rapturous glory
For lovers in their merriment true!

Oh, to be but an average person
Not as this fool in the night
To find me a slot in society
And not draw these lines in a fight—
To give me my keys to sanity
And burn all these words of the blue
And bury my pen by the moonlight
And relinquish the desire that I knew!

As time moves on to the morrow
I know that I'm out all alone
By pages and pages of misery
And by words and their rhymes in a song.
I know I can't least escape them
They're all in my tears in my glass
Wherever I pour out the bottle
They come back to haunt in my past!

Some say that the poet's a damn fool
Some say we're lazy and mean
But, oh, to be that average person
Down by the running cold stream
To find life's pleasures in measure
And give the "wide berth" to the hearse
And never, ever, dream of Kansas
And the Wizard of Oz and the worst!

THIS DAY IN INFAMY

This day in infamy
Amid the thunderous roar
In blacken, death-like skies
Through whence the fury tore—
There t'was thrown a challenge
To each of us who call
Our blessed, sacred nation
God's greatest best of all!

On that memorable morning
Among the pools of red
Through burned-out ships that lay
Are men and women—our dead.
By prophecy in some annual
God's will shall forth be done
And all our hearts and cares
Shall find the battle's won!

In war and conflicts challenge
As smoke doth clear the scene
As men and women lay still
Amid the enemy's sting,
Our nation, our blessed country,
Hath opened up its soul
And bled its sacred teardrops
Upon God's golden scroll!

As darkness starts to fade
By dawn's dim, creeping light,
The battle hath just begun
As America and soldiers fight.
For all our firm resolve
We each hath drawn in place
Shall triumph in God's end
And find its rightful faith!

As we bid them well
Our soldiers march off to war
As children spread their daisies
Before our nation's door.
Our best, our loving all,
Hath commenced to fight for home
And right the devil's rue
And move our nation on!

In fleeting days as this
As tears and heartaches fly
Before time's great hereafter,
We carry our nation's pride
And bear out God's great will.
His script He penned in hand
And give Him all our hearts
And fight on Normandy's sand!

As we love our nation
And children go off to school
As preachers draw God's flocks
Into Christ's bleeding wound,
Our hearts and all our minds
Shall be right there with those—
Those who gave their lives away
For country and for soul!

This day in infamy
As blood flows from the fight
As men and women go off
To stand up for what's right,
Our prayers and every thought
Shall follow them on to quest
And find their peaceful solace
And be God's greatest best!

As we love our country
And doves soar high above
As tears flow down the cheeks
Of those who lost their loved,
God's hand shall rightly hold
We each and lead us fair
Into His great hereafter
And comfort all our cares!

In war and pressing times
As darkness covers Earth
As tanks and guns fight on
Throughout Earth's fragile turf,
We lest hold each to truths
To all what God hath said
And raise our prayers to Him
Before our fallen dead!

As we give our hearts
To those of us who cry
For each lost cherished member
God gave His Son to die
And through our bleakest battles
God gave us all His love
To draw us close to Him
And triumph high above!

This day in infamy
As tears flow from the rage
As men and women give
Their lives in battle's wage
We each look toward our God
And His own Greatest Son
And give our hearts to Him
To collect what peace hath won!

VICTORY IN THE PERSIAN GULF
(A Tribute to America's Fighting Men and Women
in Our Armed Forces and Their Families)

They were called to duty by the acts of an aggressive foe. Our men and women took heed of a dictator's ruthless thrust into a peaceful country. Where they are needed, our Armed Forces will go. Whether it be upon the sands of Africa or whether it be in some alien land, our men and women of America's Armed Forces will be there. They are the ones who give their all. They are the proud guardians of our land born unto freedom and sanctified by God Almighty's blessings—our gallant soldiers upon some distant shore. They are the ones who give to each and everyone of us the sacred right to live under the auspicious of freedom and security.

Our blessed men and women fought the best of fights and drove a cowardly dictator from a friendly ally. Those darkest hours our brave ones fought, they triumphed over the crimes and sins of Saddam Hussein. They put their might and fury upon that evil country and taught those aggressors that crimes they had committed shall all be set right under justice and before all the eyes of this world.

Our brave ones have met their objectives and won. They have been on the shores of Tripoli; they have been in those halls of Montezuma. Where destiny calls, our brave ones shall go. Whether to give food and aid to a starving peoples or whether to rescue some tearful lost soul upon the mighty oceans, our brave men and women will go. As centuries come and go, so will our mighty Forces. As long as America exists so will the power within our land and within our hearts.

Our blessed country of freedom's torch and justice is for each and everyone of us. We Americans stand tall and proud as we gaze Earth's fragile peace. We must always be on our guard less some foolish country take up arms against a peaceful nation. We must be well prepared as the centuries hold many, many surprises for Earth's peoples. We cannot foresee what the devil may try to inflict upon God's great land—these United States of America.

And those—those who did not make it back to our American shores—they are the ones who paid the supreme price. They are the men and women to whom we reverently owe our all, our freedoms, our very lives. God bless those brave soldiers who ultimately gave their all. All the tributes in this old world cannot call them back. All our tears and words shall never draw them into our arms again. God bless those brave men and women who died so that all of us might endure with freedom's glorious blessings.

As times come and go, so will America's fighting men and women of our Armed Forces—whether they be on the ground, in the skies, or on or beneath the sea. They are the ones to whom we praise. For if it were not for our Armed Forces of these United States, tyranny might engulf the world. God forbid that! We pray to God Almighty for our soldiers of America! To them we owe our thanks and to them we shall never, ever, be able to repay them for what they've done!

God bless them one and all!!!

DIVINE CREATION

THE SKY, THE SEA
AND LITTLE MORTAL ME
INTRIGUED BY EARTH
FROM BORN OF INFINITE BIRTH.
THIS MAN, THIS FLESH,
GIVEN GOD'S LOVING BEST
ENTRENCHED WITH LOVE
SENT DOWN FROM HEAVEN ABOVE!

THIS MAN, THIS LAND,
DRAWN OUT FROM DUST AT HAND
BY HIM WHO SAVES
THIS WORLD OF SIN AND RAGE.
GOD'S SON WHO DIED
NOW RESIDES IN HEAVEN'S SKIES
AND GAVE THIS EARTH
HIS GLORY AND HIS WORTH!

LASTING ROLES

The enormity of time swallows each and every rich man's holdings. Their "precious" riches are cast away under a pile of rubble and dissolution. But some poor poet's heartfelt verse, which was once disregarded and shunned time and again, shall surface from out the legends of the years. It shall triumphantly last and endure throughout time's infamous rampage and shall pull two young hearts together in God's lasting, eternal ways... .

TURNING HOME

Knock, knock the door tis open
My windows are raised and freed
And the dark green curtains by my couch
Are drawn so that all may see.
The wind tis blowing behind my back
And God's seas are full of foam,
For the ship that took my family "home"
Shall board my soul with song!

The stars in the heavens glow for this night
To light my road through space
And the candle that burned by my bed
Has melted before death's face.
The miles and miles once tread man's feet
Are but God's eternal path
Through time and the infinite gardens so green
And through earth's painful wrath!

The clock in the tower strikes once its note
And man's hearse tis long and black
And the journey through child with its innocent smiles
Shall haunt the ones mourning in black.
This poet tis left Earth's realm of rhyme
And boarded the sonnet's trail
Through pages of prolific nursery rhymes
Through heaven and almighty hell!

The distance between the stars some say
Shall never once be filled,
And the lonely howl of some distant wolf
Shall terrify and send a chill.
Through the rhymes that filled those castle halls
Where Presidents that once had read—
There lies God's prophecies in all its alarm
Stretched out on a cold-scented bed!

The apparition of the hour at hand
Tis presiding over the feast
Upon that vengeful cold-swept morn
While raindrops cleansed and swept.
All knowledge from man's mystic brain
Which rhymed those years away
Upon God's awesome, mercy seat
Has seen this poet pray.

The years pass slowly for Earth's young
And children have their fun
While wars and upheavels and mighty lords
Contest for the love and the gun.
Those rhymes which bridged God's heavens and stars
Are but a millenium away,
Far from the madden aggravation of earth
That turned toward home today!

THERE IS A GOD

There is a God out there.
He's as alive as the honeysuckle on the vine.
He's as real as the birth of a young fawn deer.
He's as vivacious as the skies high above some endless plain.
There is a God. His mirrored picture is in the noise
Of the running brook. His tears of joy are as real
As the spring's melting snow.
His compassion is as consoling as a mother's love
For her innocent, young child.
There is a God out there.
His beauty is as real as the stars in the heavenly firmament.
His voice can be heard from every church podium
Throughout this great land.
His values are as true as the wonderous balance of nature.
There is a God out there.
His poets are as disciples to His unfinished business.
His "word-phrasers" are as true to their souls
As mortal man can be and His works are as
Earth's love gifts from His great, large generous heart... .

RESIGNED TO DEATH

I am resigned to my death as a lily is
To wilt upon that ebony frozen plain
Where teardrops no more drip
Where lie the sane and insane
And the embark of soul and heart
Shall silence me through death's dark.
Once I had hoped to play—
And meditate wonderful ways
Of contemplating my golden age
With a child into my lap.
Her golden hair so bright
To warm and cheer my songs
And renew an interest far gone
Cause the Gods know by now
That as winter creeps into earth's breast
And sickness ramparts the mote,
That I, the ambivalent poet,
Should resign my script to the young—
The young who share the zest and flame
But aren't as daring and apt to proclaim,
For as a dark bird serenades the nest
And hovers the arena of my bed
And closes its beak with a hideous snear,
My blood shall cease its rampart flow.
Red shall stain earth's new fallen snow
And as the little songbird that sang its tune,
I shall wither on that limb
Thrust bluntly into some tomb.
For the nails on my hands shall continue to grow,
All will be macabre and time will then slow.
Another's daisy shall bloom in that spring
And all the markers will gradually age.
Oh, God, what hath spring now done?
The weeds have begun their creep over my bed—
That vine t'was made for honeysuckle and bloom.

But now tis covering the words of my tomb—
Those words that told of merriment and jest
Have all been silenced by death and the rest.
Oh, look—a soul tis next to my plot
The one that cursed me before my throb stopped
That enemy that threatened the house where I lived
Tis living next door and doing Lucifer's will
Next to my bedside in those final days
And wringing his hands as though he'd get paid.
That God, in some void, which governed my flight
Has long since forgotten our deal in the night.
The crowd has all gone and nothing but dirt
Lies piled high atop some eternal sleep's berth.
The wreaths are all scented and some are still green
They wreak of an odor which permeates the scene.
Alas, the box all cushioned with silk
Weathers the ground in my cold, camp plight.
The stars are all gone and there's nothing but night
The next spring's breath brings the clover and grass.
The daisies have blossomed and covered the past.
My body put away not one soul thinks twice
For earth is occupied with living, ah how nice.
Oh, but for a moment to spend in the sun
With the orchids that smell of love and spring's fun.
All have vanished in some terrible night—
All have forgotten this ambient sight... .
Yes, I am resigned to my death
As a lily is to wilt
Upon that ebony, frozen plain
Where teardrops no more drip—
Where lie the sane and insane,
And the embark of soul and heart
Shall silence me through death's dark!

LOVE'S COSMOS

A sense of awe, the great beyond
Summoned my mind of male.
It pierced my soul this night of old
And set my horizons to sail.

To sail through the vastness of a time
Through the long corridors of life
Through the chambers of the gods
And took my soul to flight.

Beyond the planets, beyond the stars
The heavens did extend their arms
And open forth a cherished amore
This night on my little farm.

For as I gaze at space and time
And at the Milky Way,
I wonder of the rays of light
That govern my every day.

I wonder of the life abroad
I sense a need to be
A lonely poet this night alive
Tis no one but me.

Tis no one but love alone
The great beyond hath said
Gaze at my way, old bruttle man,
Thy wretched being in bed.

I looked and looked and spied my star
A speck of light so true,
And stared and shared that night impaired
And found my love t'was you.

NON-STOPPING POEM

I am a slave to the rhyme
No matter how bad it hurts
No matter how sharp the sting
No matter how long the hearse.

A memento I scratch as follows,
"This life hath seen me fly
Through happiness, grief, and serious ponder—
Oh, when shall these teardrops die"?

The sky shall swell its damp clouds
To saturate the lines I have drawn
And eat away at my lyrics
Till all is left but bones.

What matter if I leave in a hurt?
My song shall bid me bye
And sprout once more in some garden in June
Till earth and the elements sigh!

CURSE OF THE POET

In early morn, the night chill lingering,
A ludicrous pen by fingers moves—
By lamp, by candle, by Devil, or God,
Hellbent by circumstance and earthly booze!

The lines wax longer in their flight
Cross miles of parchment from birth to grave—
A poet spills forth his tears of madness,
As an erratic, despondent, outcast slave!

Prattle tales, sweet lullabies, and melodious slangs
Are scribbled with blood from grim and bare—
The saints shall deny and curse the one
Who jots the lines and pulls his hair!

Oh, God—thy Creator of perfect prose,
Why charge this poet of despairing lay—
By grit, guts, why or where,
To rhyme his lyrics this delirious way!

WAR'S RED ROSE

She had eyes of a sapphire, her cheeks were rose red,
Her lips were as a ruby, and her hair was golden-spread;
She was all my woman and all my lass of heart,
For she was on my mind in the war-scared battle's dark.

The whistle bombs grew louder, the rockets' tone welled on
And somewhere in that night I hummed myself a song;
A song of red, red roses and of a girl I knew,
Little did I know that night my life was almost through.

My watch showed almost eleven, the fight had barely started;
Somewhere to my left, a paramedic had darted
For boys were dying fast and blood was flowing free.
It was now up to us to save our liberty.

Yes, Johnson was on the hill, Johnson was at his ranch
Beer-busting the elite, laughing at some dance;
He was safe and sound in my hell of night.
About that time a shot tore me as a knife.

There I lay a-bleeding, red, oh, Dad, you see
Just like that red, red rose in her hair across the sea;
Just like my warm-hearted woman, her lips so rosy red
I lay there a-dying, my gut now openly spread.

And as the minutes passed, the trail of red moved on,
On to a fairer land where my lass, my love had gone,
On to a distant horizon, on to a beautiful world;
Her red, red rose I became that night, never again to see my
girl.

CONFESSION

As this night passes with its turbulent infatuation of the gods, mad ink graces sacred parchment as endowing thoughts are laid to rest for all the times to behold. The world, though caught up in its volatile eruptions upon desolute days, has all the monumental folkways laid out and immortalized by striving savages from its dark cold past.

God's sun will break over the nations of this Earth as this fool's mind hath closed out all recognition of average, sensible works and hath engrossed his ludicrous thoughts upon a time and a place that never shall be realized. As the long, hideous hours doth pass and the noise of the clock hath turned to but a whisper, the stringent, ambivalent craving for rhyme and rhythm hath dominated this simple room and holds no grudge for the "erks" of this demon with his pen.

Those latitudes, given in all resentment, are the forces which move and promote this fool's adulterous affection for the thoughts which cause traumatic affections with God's clean, clear night air. As if some strange, bizarre attraction hath cancelled all human furloughs, this creature transverses through the "propagated millenniums" as though by his own admission and damnful desire—a blight in his own eyes and temporal lobe shuts out all disillusions which foster his indeterminable understanding of the word, rest.

As fall draws to a close and the quest for winter tis but a stone's throw into some boiling sea of dejection, this savage labors upon his disgust and euphoric desire to silence the "bipolar" affections which drive and propel him to the point of no returning to those normal realms of life and complacency. The aroraious crowds doth cast laughter upon this poet's agonized escapades into that interlude that permeates all elapsed time of perfidious betrayals of the word poet.

Some archaic gesture comes from this creature's frail mind as he parts with his embryonic sanity which never fully developed before rampant thoughts and delirious hallucinations invaded his soul and struck him down in the midst of depression and grandeur. The effectiveness accumulations of rhyme and risque script hath incarcerated his ascertained dialogue into some scholar's impetuous nightmare.

As belligerent to the warming winds, which tell of impending disaster ahead, this wreckless prophet of gloom and doom fights his way among carnivorous predators and escapes once again that fatal rendezvous with the eternal abyss. As evening approaches and ebony shadows cast their eerie glare upon this poet's soul, an evil metamorphisis permeates through susceptible, emulated hostilities and a craving for sanity and acceptance looms before this creature's red eyes. The wind and God's thunderous heavens sound out their fury warning that all tis not well in that diastrophism of movement upon planet Earth.

The itinerary of this poet's soul, lurking just beyond some maelstrom in the most treacherous waters, has all but given its formable signal to begin if not for some magnanimous pull to the halls of the great and the noble. Kings and Queens come and go; Presidents and Senators rise and fall and those invidious apemen known only as australopithecine can fathom what the tomorrow shall bring and lay before our vindictive lots on this ole planet.

Those pillars of Hercules shall crumble to dust and ruin as the demanding elements of environmental upheavel and earthly war draw upon their ceaseless resources and take away and destroy what little advancement sapiens have made throughout these fleeting decades. This poet's pen shan't bridge the widening gap separating heaven's portals from corruption and blasphemous evil that blights every living creature upon the spherical mass we call our home. Every living organism which craves on nourishment shall one day have his or her final encore before the stars in God's endless void.

As I draw to a close this humble verse, I thank God for the opportunity of being able to live and love and be as all life can be—short, brief, and longing for that special place of euphoria. I know man will never remember these words that I have confessed this cold, fridged November night. As I stand before my final rhythm and as my pen's ink seemingly runs out, I look for the solace promised in perfect serenity long ago.

My God which gave me His gift of the rhyme will, in all honesty and forth-righteousness, give me His pen to a new script—one that has never-ending ink and one that carries the rhyme drawn from the heart and not by the hand. For, as my heart speaks in all its God-fearing reverence and loving charity, there also will be my soul.....

DEAREST LOVE

As this seemingly grateful lad hath been drawn to thou wonderful ways, I can reason with the gods that every minute I am with thee tis but pure joy and enlightment. Oh, Lassie, thou memories are of some elated trance upon the bosom of this blissful night which thou hast cast my undeserving way. As time doth propagate through the millenniums of some grateful, translucent light-year, thou radiance hath pulled my wainful thoughts to thou precious side.

Thou presence hath embossed my heart strings with the chorus of thy beautiful, charming halo and run rampant through my starving heart forevermore. Thou beauty tis of the fairer meadow. Thou wonderful presence hath caused the lilies to bloom forth and the daisies and clover to cover my inner soul with warmth, love, and Christian understanding.

Thou caring ways hath drawn nigh towards some unrelenting, majestic lure and propelled my tearful heart-throb straight into thou life and charity and precious occupancy of thou inner soul. As the fool doth move over the face of almighty beauty and fails to see and grasp its presence, this pitiful poet in earth's cold night doth reason by his sheer instincts that God hath made a place for thee into my life and fleeting folkways.

If all the mountains turn to mere rubble, if all the seas of this earth run dry, I shallest never forsake thou glowing radiance and I will never forget the infatuate impression that thou hath made into my mind and heart. As love letters in God's night must surely end, and, as the dreams—the hopes and the aspirations of a more perfect and sincere world are manifested throughout this "spherical mass" called earth—I shall never once forsake thee.

In closing, I might add that as my soul and life shall someday go to meet the Eternal Matchmaker in the heavenly firmament,

William Furr

I shallest never be drawn to a more perfect and beautiful lassie than the joy I see in thou. I shall never forget the humble feelings and transformations I have experienced these last timely days. I shall never, ever, once take any amount of remuneration for all the happy, wonderful feelings that thouest hath brought into my rhythm and rhyming soul.

God bless thee, beautiful lassie, and may the enormity of Fathertime hold each and every "love-beam" from thee and propel them straight into the heart and bosom of this grateful and sincere lad. I love thee, my angel!

Love,

THE MOST WONDERFUL GIRL IN THE WORLD

She pranced about fancy
Her hair a scarlet red;
Her skin was of the fairest,
Her eyes told she was wed.
My poise demeaned by her walk;
Oh, God! my soul askew.
The years pass long and weary
For poetry that is true!

That angel of all time and infamy
God's lift to a heavy heart;
While moonbeams rake upon a sea
Once tread by Noah's ark.
Times blitz through the archives of ages
Christ's angel to comfort my soul.
Why, if not for that heavenly female,
The days wax dark and so cold!

The solace, the haven, the garden
A refuge from turbulent times;
The armies of all Earth's Caesars
Shan't waiver her heart or her mind;
While wrinkles creep o'er my fleshtones
And lilies turn dark with some blight.
Her radiance shines through the stillness
And resurrects in a superlative might!

William Furr

The rebellious, the sinners, the pity
Were all flung far from her tranquil scene;
While time and the infinite mortals
Played host to their glorious queen.
I know by a hair and a silkthread
I cling on in my miserable words
But if not for the awesome memories
Of the most wonderful girl in the world!!!

WHAT IS A POEM???

A poem is the sum deposit of all our hopes, dreams, and aspirations subtracted from our doubts, fears, and uncertainties and carried over to a higher power. A poem is work music for the human soul and saving grace for the bleeding spirit. A poem is logic for the human mind and irresistible curiosity for the sacred heart. It is the absolute for all our goals and the zenith for all our attainable highs.

A poem is like manna from the sky, dew drops on Easter roses and milk from out the bosom of Mother Earth for all starving peoples. A poem is to mankind what sheep are to the shepherd—what the rainbow is to the sky and what daisies are to the fairer meadow.

A poem is food for thought to the scholar's demeanor and appetite for the nourishment of the fruits of plenty and cooling liquid to the parched tongue. A poem is the lily to the tranquil pond. It is the sun to the darken earth, and it is the courage to be truthful and honest.

A poem is of some sacred trust. It is to give and to give and never think about receiving. A poem is to love—to be loved and to care enough about mortal man more than your own self. A poem is a gift. It is as God's fresh breath of spring. It is those long hot summery days all filled with love and happiness and special good times together.

A poem is like God's majestic fall shedding not its leaves but its special true feelings and covering mankind with caring, sharing, and a new pledge of commitment and understanding.

William Furr

And, last, a poem is like a voice from heaven—confronting some tearful, grateful word-slave night after night and day after day. A poem is straight from the bosom of God Almighty. It is His answer to boredom and His eternal gift of rhyme and amazing grace for all who would only ask...
.

A REASON

For every minute ant that crawls across a single grain of
sand—
There is a reason.
For every robin that feeds life into its fresh born young—
There is a reason.
As the sky folds back and emits the lights of stars billions of
years old—
There is a reason.
And as fools as I scribble their haunting convictions night
after
Night amid the noise and whispers of mankind—
There most definitely is a "grand plan" by which it all came
about.
The stars in the heavenly firmament seemingly dance and
twinkle
To the rhythm of our God many, many light years from our
Earthly bosoms.
As time and fools, as I, mingle hand and hand, wit to wit,
And word to word under God's infamous presence, may
some
Doubting brother or sister seeking high ground upon the
rock see
And believe the earnest rhymes I pen sincerely this late
September's night.
As armies rise and fall, as kingdoms build and destruct, and
As the ceaseless cries of the young and old alike ring
haunting
Dialogues through our troubled souls, may God Almighty
understand His creation—man.
May God's eternal presence upon the universe's "hanging
balance"
Of forces guide and steer all life away and back from its fall
Towards eternal chaos and self-annihilation.
I shall close with the simplest words I know how and end
this

Soul-searching script amid the dawn of a new earth day.
There most definitely is a reason for it all and that reason is
The same reason a fool, such as I, am allowed to voice his
Tearful utterances upon his conscious night after night.
God cares—and with that one thought in mind amid the
"seas and valleys"
of mortal doubts and fears, I rest assured, as I fight
With the flight of my pen that my God truly tis love… .

ALL AND ALL

Upon the ebony, wind-blown night
With crystallizing jewels aglow
From depths no mortal hath ever once been
There comes time's awesome show
With twinkling lights upon God's space
And the grandest chore all done
Our hearts shall lure our souls to rest
And seek eternity's Son!

From out man's pitiful, unconscionable quests
And into dawn's first glow
There in all time's rapturous splendor
Now lies a heavenly show
God's harps are played by angel bands
And all death hath gone away
For all tis left but joy on high
And Jesus every day!

In our quagmires scornful place
We humans chance our tears
And weep upon time's forever rock
This earth throughout our years.
We chalice poets of our lost rhymes
Hath lived to see the day
Beauty! For our own enjoy
And Jesus by our way!

The eternal quest born out of old
And the trillions of miles intend
All t'wer given God's one who braved
Evil and all its sins.
For we who hold the Judgement Book
And never, ever, once read
We shall surely dust if off
When Christ shall intercede!

The starry sky above our brows
And millions and billions of lights
And every now a comet's trail
Doth lure our hearts to sight.
For as our souls hath stood in test
We humans never once quence
Our hearts shall be our eternal gauge
Which God hath right intend!

As poets ponder verse on verse
And try to rhyme the night
All creation's wonderful glories fair
Share our eternal plites.
For God shall pull us up from mire
All right our wayward souls
Upon time's forever, endless quest
Throughout his grandest roles!

Infatuated with the "zeal" of things
And perplexed beyond our times
We humans frail with star-struck souls
Hath seen God's spiritual rhymes.
For all He is and all He was
And what He is to be
Enormity! Grandest! Forever kind!
Jesus!!! Endlessly!!!

We little meek-like "men of Rome"
And scholars upon "Mar's Hill"
And Scribes and Pharisees doubting whims
Are but some fleeting frills.
For all that was and all that is
And all there is to be
Shall include us in God's wonderous works
With Jesus!!!   Eternity!!!

ALL OF US

The irresistible sky, wide in view
And the ocean's roaring surf
And little, small, timid birds that fly
Above God's bountiful earth
All hath drawn the songs of man
To expound with grateful hearts
Oh, God! The Greatest, Wondrous One
Oh, Christ! How great Thou art!

The awing lure of distant lights
And darkness upon the deep
An eternal space that stretches away
Forever from out God's feast
Gives right we humans in frail-like trance
Our songs to rhyme those works
And lets us thank God for His grace
From out Christ's saving worth!

Earth's highest mountains steep in slope
And deserts that stretch away
And life abound from out this land
Shows us God paid that way.
For each small love we cast His way
And each small life lived true
Shall come back in God's form of love
This world and all we, too!

The infinite lives that berth in time
As billions of stardust flew
And never-ending songs of God
Tell man our Lord tis true.
For by His acts upon the scene
He loved us by our ways
And caused the boundless, everlasting time
To include us in His days!

Earth's deepest oceans born with life
With watery abyss depths
And rainbows in the endless skies
Show all what God bequeathed.
For all tis for us to enjoy
And reap His harvest true
And sow our seeds with righteous deeds
And know God loves us, too!

The thundering herds of wildest beasts
And droves of birds that fly
And rolling hills with hollows fair
Show us God doth reside.
For man shan't grasp the "all" of things
He never held the sun
Nor earth, nor moon, nor starbeams sent
Except God's Righteous One!

We place Christ in our souls to bear
Our weakest and our ways
And pray to God up in His sky
And thank Him for our days.
For as the stars hang o'r our heads
And angels sing in peace
We man upon this aging earth
Shall reap God's harvest feast!

As time rolls on in infinite speed
And heavenly bodies fly
Far out from creation's sacred bliss
Our God doth love us nigh.
For what we choose to pave our way
Into His eternal home
Shall rightly be the Son of Man
JESUS!   FOR OUR OWN!!!

BE PERSISTANT
(Work and Finish Your Dream)

Have you, in your lows, quit a task
And dropped th' chore at hand?
Or, have you floundered in a sea
Of diminished persistance and ran???

Whether your wash be half dried in the sun
Or your house is half-way clean—

Be persistant in the hour at hand—
"Praise God—and work for the dream"!

What if the work is drudgerous and long?
A "work completed,"—tis music to the soul.
Have you ever realized how good a feeling
To see the results—Behold!!

The bird doesn't stop till its work is completed
Neither does the tall sturdy oak;
What matters in the long run—is,
How vocal you sang every note!!

Whether night or day or high amongst the stars
Whether poor or glorious like a king,

Time never pauses, nor God, save none—
So—"work and finish your dream"!!!

THE BEST IS YET TO COME

This is the age for doers;
This is the age for work.
Man must take the challenge
And till the fertile Earth,
For God won't mind the plow ruts
Nor the innocent evening's fun,
For man and angels and the Almighty
The best is yet to come!

From the lovely village steeples
To the congested city I know,
Man's traffic takes on new roads
And crosses a herd of doe.
From the boundless, endless blue skies
With planets weighing many-a-ton
God shall accentuate His brushstrokes
For the best is yet to come!

The short-spaced stage we work from,
Its curtain rises but once
And there's never any intermission
Just bring your ticket and lunch.
We build upon our families
And rest not till chores be done;
We live and breath and love God,
For the best is yet to come!

The hungry child shall have food;
The "least" shall have their "fill",
For man must strive with the angels
To remove and correct Earth's ills.
Our church is one but many
Where Christians can be one;
And never hoard the talents,
For the best is yet to come!

The little, sweet, wholesome babies;
The elderly gentle souls
And all around us love life
Created just for His fold.
The Master puts the finishs
Upon His Beloved Son
And draws on many a pleasure,
For the best is yet to come!

We hear all around us heartbeats
Crying out for the love,
And we see the small, fresh daisies
Beneath the high flying dove.
For God and man and Earth-town
Shall rejoice when the time has come
And speed into the infinite heavens,
For the best is yet to come!!!

CHRISTIANS AND THE COMING OF THE MESSIAH

Prophet to earth's war-scarred pages
Helmsman in man's perilous seas;
The humble ecclesiastic of ages
Casts serenity on a dischanter as me—

Come from that diatribe gray-sky
Away from the dreadful grave

The dream of all the aeons
The hope of all the saved!

Torn by heaven and earth's time strands
Nailed on a naked rod;
Tormented by mockery and ridicule,
Spat upon as though sod.

Ay, the child shall come home to its master
The Christians shall come home to their Christ

And the workers of all the wicked
Shall reap the devil's vice!

Not shackled by Caesar's infidelities,
Not confused by a perilous sea;
Christ shall drown man's problems in due time
When He comes for you and for me.

Those charlatans in the thick of their seances
Earth's atheists who live for the glee—

And all the wicked and blasphemers
Shall wail and fall down on their knees!

Mary's rivers of tear-drops "a'shedeth"
Paul's blood which poured from the "blade";
And all Peter's sorrows and heartaches
Shall afix to the scales and be weighed—

For such are the maths for the measure
And measure will have in due time

The total of all Christ's children
As they fling to the skies in a rhyme!

Honey will flow from the sepulchers
For lives shall be resurrected by the tons
And never the flock shall waiver,
For Christ hath returned and hath won—

For the sword hath been beaten into plowshares
And the grapes in the vineyards shall spiral

Into God's infinite domain
Which stretches for billions of miles!

The stammering, dumb, and neglected;
The pauper, the widower, and me
And all our countless brethren
Shall awake in heaven and be—

As a child presses close to its mother
We, too, shall press close to our Lord.

And adorn His head with our ointment
And never, no never, be bored!

For—as wine spills forth from the creekbeds,
As gold dust lines the sea
Heaven's serene and personified tranquility
We Christians, together, shall be—

Much mindful of all our blessings
And grateful to a steadfast love

For the Jesus to whom we come
Is the Jesus to whom we love!!!

--End

COLLECTION OF LITTLE HEARTS

As sweet as a flower's scent
And perfect as some rhyme
Our little hearts give back to us
Our God and love in time.
For as they gather around our sides
Our hearts are moved with love
All glory spilt in rapturous time
Shall move our souls above!

Our little hearts are pure and sweet
They want to hold our hands
And tell us of the Sandman's trip
From the night at hand.
From innocent little words they say
To all the love of man
Their little lives hath "made our day"
Just what God hath planned!

Our love for our little ones
Hath all but blessed God's day
With love and peace and Christ's own kind
In His own glorious way.
For as my aging hand with pen
Draws all these words I choose
So shall God right bless them all
His best! He hath include!

As little hearts must all grow up
Into some older rage
And time and place hath all erased
The poet's grave and page.
God's blessed ones from out His work
Reflect His peace of heart
And warm our souls throughout our time
And bless us with His art!!!

COME HOME
(A Song)

When all the tears are dried—
When all the leaves have fallen—
When all the armies have gone—
And when all "earth's souls" are home—

What then, oh, God, in your heavens?
What then shall you do with your man???
Shall you plant him in heavenly gardens
And raise him as righteous as you can???

Oh, Lord, in your highest of places—
Oh, God, let us dwell not alone—
Come render us worthy of thy presence—
Come guide us on to Thy throne.

Those tears have dried in this poem
And the leaves are covered with snow.
My army has all but dismantled
And my soul has lost all its woe.
The heart has loosened its body
And the mind has shed all its pain;
For as surely as I write this last sonnet
My world tis no longer the same.

Oh, Lord, in Your highest of places—
Oh, God, let us dwell not alone—
Come render us worthy of Thy presence—
Come guide us on to Thy throne.

The night and the blights have all vanished
And this agonizing fool has come home
To an encore of beautiful music
And to a Christ that can carry His own!

DESTINY

--written for Dr. Bobby Douglas
and all God's children at
First Baptist Church

We rendezvous with destiny
Amid God's farthest stars
Way out by Gabriel's glory
From birth to death we start.
Entrenched we follow starlight
Each ray with hope and cheer
To find our God residing
Beyond our shedding tears!

As dawn breaks forth the nightly chill
And stars fade into space
Our Mighty God with all His love
Hath given this world His grace.
Those things we hold and strive to keep
Are but some earthly pleasure;
Those things t'wer born into our souls
Are time's eternal treasure!

Mankind as we can spill our thoughts
And cast our pens along
Time's memorable, undaunting, trying span
And word our rhymes with song.
But wait! Those little truths we know
Are still God's wonderous signs.
They stand in awe and glorify
His never-ending line!

The indulging crowds of earthly host
Crave the taste of wine
And scorn what they cannot believe
And jest in foolish rhyme.
But all of us of Christian faith
Who call ourselves our Lord's
Shall find our destiny greater than
The sinners all accord!

God's endless time from which we view
Is an eternal, forever sign
Of suns and moons upon the deep
In never-ending rhyme.
And great are His explicit notes
God strung upon His harp.
He put to rest our fears and doubts
With His great, generous heart!

As time doth move into some space
Of scars and aging haste
And we wax upon this earth
And greet our impending faiths.
We, who love our Greatest One,
Shall look and see our cue
To enter God's grandest, wonderous house
And live and start anew!

Those who love the souls of man
And speak God's righteous words
Upon this earth with lives to care
And give us saving words.
They shall one day grasp the hand
Of He who set us free
Upon our faith's forever lives
With Christ and destiny.

The moon-cast sky with ebony deep
And starlight upon our face
And woods and water and wealth galore
Are all God's mighty grace.
For destiny with our impending time
Shall greet our greatest cheer
Of Jesus and heavenly, endless love
FOREVER AND A YEAR!!!

THE ETERNAL FLAME
(A Love of Country)

As elegant as the soaring eagle
That guards our country's skies,
As eternal as the endless brook
Whose waters flow us by,
A torch t'was lit with precious blood
And hoisted to the wind.
Oh, God! Let us not least forget
How freedom first began!

Burn on, burn on,
Oh torch that lit the sky;
Many men of every state of rank
Hold awe their very eyes.
Upon thou glowing freedom's torch
That came by pain and cries
Let us not forget our gallant boys
Who carried it on to die.

The rapturous beat of war and strife
Echoes upon some field
Where men of right ensued to fight
And save all freedom's will.
The blood they spilt enhanced that flame
From out the burning torch
It lit the skies while soldiers died
To them we do rejoice!

The distant cannons echo thrice
A rumbling tis in the air
Of shouts and yells and earthly hell
Of blood and deathly stares.
From out this night of past-gone lives
Our freedom's flame lives on
To them we owe our very breath
To them I rhyme this song!

The land tis quiet in a hush
As morning brings its song
Of children with their precious hearts
And old men in their homes.
A price t'was paid for a sight
As freedoms such as these
I rhyme this simple heartfelt verse
Upon my trembling knees!

God's eagle soars above the land
And earth tis now at rest
Upon some quiet-hushed lily pond
The day gives forth its best.
And poets search their longing souls
For rhymes to honor "them"—
Those boys that gave their precious lives
So freedom may live again!

Burn on, burn on
Oh torch that lit the sky;
May men of every state of rank
Hold awe their very eyes.
Upon thou glowing freedom's torch
That came by pain and cries
Let us not forget our gallant boys
Who carried it on to die!!!

ETERNAL SUN

The great born zeal of burning sun
Hath broken earth's fragile crest
Above time's endless, boundless space
And shows our Lord at best.
Those rays of light are, too, of hope
A promise that sets us free
From out the night's cold chill now gone
Upon some passing spree.

This eternal scene from out God's rhyme
Above the hearts of man
From centuries past and looming works
Shows God hath drawn His plan.
The treacherous sea with all its wrecks
From eternity to this page
All hold the dreams of past-gone kings
And bring God front to stage.

Above my simple heartfelt writ
And through some humble lore
God Almighty hath charged my pen
To scribe my soul and score.
From shackled and impoverished sin
My heart shall leap so free
And garner up those things that last
Christ!   And eternity!

The hands of Father time it seems
Hath moved through early day
From wars and kingdoms wrought with men
And through some poets "lay".
Those fleeting hours which hold our worth
Shall one day each one be
The gauge of all eternity's woe
From out God's endless fee.

As moving through some sacred sky
God's sun now warms our day
From out the morn's cold chill at large
Our hearts doth move its way.
We ponder whence it shall soon bring
Our wants, our hopes, our cards
For little do we feel the sign
Of glory in God's air!

Some old and tired and lonely soul
Into his pitiful plight
Shall see God's wonderful, timeless moves
Upon His soul's delight.
For He tis loved by eternity's best
And He shall one day see
A Son far greater than this sky
Above time's endless sea!

This writer hath been moved by God
To pen what holds his sight
From earthly form in deepest faith
Our hearts hath felt God's might.
For as our bodies mold away
And as our tears grow old
God Almighty shall pave that way
Into His Book of Souls!

Time's eternal glow throughout the sky
And systems far and wide
And billions and billions of past-gone rhymes
Are all God's finest kinds.
For each and every line we draw
Unto God's generous wage
Shall be His lasting, endless love
From out our tear-soaked page!!!

THE ETERNAL SURF

Moving as the waves of time
Hath churned God's mighty seas
From out this earthly life He bore
The surf doth come so free.
For, lo! The very lure of space
Hath all seen tides come in
God's boundless, eternal, endless nights
Are filled right to the brim!

God's planets far in distant space
Are held in depths of time
And tears of all man's pitiful works
Are all past tense in rhyme.
For lights from out the eternal void
Hath all relinquished free
And set our rhythmic trails to fly
By God!—Through eternity!

Time's mighty pull towards distant place
Hath all evoked man's mind
To gaze and wonder through eons spent
Where shall we berth in time!!
To what we owe this sacred space
We share in living lines??
And where hath come God's own delights
His stars in forever rhyme???

The awesome power of boundless love
From out our meager stance
And the very provoked debts of verse
Are all God's timeless trance.
For all are held in hallowed grace
All are by some right
God's own grand, wonderous, loving signs
Are here by His great might!

Upon this earth we wax in vain
Through our own miserable toils
And garner up what bread we cleave
And plod earth's miring soil.
But far above our wretched heads
God's sky tis as our dreams
His timeless, ceaseless, beautiful surf
From out His eternal scene!

As man and savage shrug their way
Through this earth's treacherous life,
God's stars high above the clouds
Press on through night after night.
For as the heavens doth rule the sky
Our God made in their birth
So shall mortal man commence
To wonder by their worth!

The rapturous dawn of infinite space
Tis far from earth in time
And systems born of billions of lights
Shall never grace our rhyme.
God's cosmic glories by the time
Our world shall be no more
Shall we evoke the will of Him
That loves us forever more!

As angels from the sands of time
Are all the glories of Him
And darkness on the face of depth
Hath God invested in.
We humans in our pious selves
Should all seek out the man
And invite Christ into our hearts
Before our hour at hand!

William Furr

From out God's stardust comes a surf
And pulls its mighty tide
Into man's vulnerable, transit verse
And leaves us as we bide.
For each and every rhyme we pen
Hath left our sands on shore
To their own moving, endless surf
Eternal and forever more!!!

FLIGHT OF THE RHYME

Beyond this planet's field of pull
Beyond the distant moon aglow
Far out from allusive thoughts of man
There lies a verse in grandest show.
Time's dominance over the scheme of all
And endless miles of raging rhyme
Doth put to test our allusive lore
And solidify the loving lines!

The mellow tears of centuries old
And mountains above some abyss deep
From angels on the highest clouds
To mankind in his daily keep
All move towards soothing, tranquil songs
That ring those words which God hath drawn
And rhyme the hymns of rhythmic swoon
To pen our best that we hath known!

Those lordly songs throughout the page
Of time's own infinite, undawning writ
And melodies which cool earth's days
Doth speed the heart which God hath sent
Toward higher bliss up in His sky
By the greatest poet from times of old
We earthlings wax upon our rage
And draw those thoughts upon our souls!

Earth's distant cannons blare with sounds
And armies rumble along life's days
And little small children still play in hand
With each fair hearts in grandest way.
But, lo, the rhyme hath bore man's soul
To pen God's eternal loving songs
Throughout this fleeting world we knew
And bring afront his endless home!

God's stars in awesome wonderment grace
His eternal firmament in grand array
And beyond this realm of mortal eyes
His deep, dark space doth stretch away
From time to depth to morn to dark
We humans plow God's endless rows
And raise those things which we hath seed
To glorify His sacred role!

Time's eons wrought with pillage rue
And death's looming hand upon our brows
Brings each we marked men by our works
To garner what we spake out loud.
For Christ alone hath paid our wage
To exemplify His grandest role
That each of us are judged wherein
We cast our lots and run our souls!

The great horizon beyond our pens
And breath to death and light to dark
And bodies beyond the frailing mind
Allude our thoughts which we embarked
For rhyming bliss tis not the gauge
Whence God shall judge our spirits nigh
Tis Christ, the Supremest, Purest One
Who holds the pen to tranquil sky!

As moments slip beyond our grasp
And years move on in fleeting roll
And age doth bring our thoughts to bear
Upon time's endless forever role.
We children in our "ceaseless plays"
Doth bring to God our longing hearts
To front His great, eternal flight
From dust to morn and death embarked!

As I draw end to my meek rhyme
Which spills those thoughts from times of old
Upon our face and through our flesh
To bear the grip into our souls.
We poets in our marvelous ways
Can bring to light our purest page
And rhyme those worlds many years apart
Our best intent throughout our rage!

God's heavens in their perspective trance
And lights born distance throughout His void
And fools and scholars without a glance
Shall never once see God's all accord.
For each small pen we mark our page
And sign away what we hath sold
Unto His grandest, endless nights
From life to death and eternal roll!!!

FREEDOM'S SONG

As sun doth lift its beaming rays
Upon God's grandest throne
He made our land as He had planned
And gave us miles to roam.
We each are His great work of art
For God hath made this soil,
This land where freedom lives and thrives
Throughout our works and toils.

Oh, America, America,
Our own great land of home
We speak of your own boundless love
Your grand skies and your songs.
We each shall find our long-sought dream
And in time we hath stood
Before God's greatest freedom's home
Throughout this land of good!

As time doth slip away with years
And our hearts long for youth
As days doth pass our fading dreams
Our God holds them in truths.
We think of all His glorious land
America! For our home!
And all those freedoms beneath His stars
To guide us as we roam.

Oh, America, America,
Your land tis what we deemed
A haven for some longing hearts
A mecca for some king.
As time doth bide our granted stance
Upon this land of home,
We all shall say she's good as gold
And claim her for our own!

156

Through years and tears of passing times
When we were young and keen,
Our rightly thoughts of God's great land
Shall see us to our King.
And as we stand before God's all
His land of freedom's bars
Our hearts shall find their solace there
With Jesus and His stars!

Oh, America, America,
This land of young and old
This haven for some longing hearts
This land of God's own fold.
Our eyes doth lift beyond the hour
And go to meet God fair
And thank Him for this grateful gift
Our land! He made with care!

As we must end our freedom's song
And as we go our ways,
We each hath taken something good
Of something God hath gave.
It tis this love throughout His land
This land God made so free
And called upon His mighty Son
To love us endlessly!

Oh, America, America,
Our hearts doth move with awe
As we reflect the heart of Him
Who died to save us all.
For we shall truly love always
God's greatest freedom's land
This country that Christ paid the way
To take us in His hands!!!

GOD ETERNAL

Behold I gazed the sunrise
As I stood upon Earth's sand,
I heard the ocean's pounding surf
And felt the breeze at hand.
As my eyes glanced towards the heavens
And the moon now dimmed by light,
I felt God's loving presence
And awed by His great might.

As morning drew its love songs
And little small birds did sing,
I sensed the endless glory
Of time's eternal King
And touched a flower by my hand
And saw its glorious bloom.
Oh, God, Thy art thy mighty
To give this poet a tune!

The day passed soft and swiftly
As men engrossed with work
Built and laid the ground stones
Of cities upon this Earth.
But a song within my heart throb
Guides me towards God's own plan
Where His Almighty presence
Shows great His infinite hand.

Now evening began to draw forth
And shadows began to spread
Upon Earth's mighty mountains
As the skies turned faintly red.
And the cool of breeze upon me
T'was all I need to know
That God t'was ever present
As dark began to show.

Now Earth tis quiet and resting
And time to end this song
By a poet so blessed with blessings
Of sea and sky and home.
And from out God's timeless star-space
Our Christ reigns from His throne
In all heaven's rapturous glory
To receive His rightful own!!!

GOD! GREAT GOD UP HIGH!

Upon this moonlit night at hand
With all its peaceful stance
There tis a God who watches all
From out His heavenly glance.
For, lo, God moved His loving hand
And born a fool as me
To word His rhymes of endless love
So all earth's men could see.

This frailing mind I hath obtained
Shall sail through sonnets fair
And all my lyrics drawn from heart
Shall one day cease their glare.
For God Almighty hath moved my pen
Unto some sacred page
And draw those truths He hath for all
And paid us each our wage.

Our Almighty Lord who reigns up high
Hath all man's best at heart
From out His boundless, endless love
He gave us each our parts
And called to me, His humble slave
Of rhymes and rhythmic lore,
To tell men of His Greatest Son
Through earth's vast life galore.

This aging hand I pen with love
Hath all those scars of life
And from out my humble, weakest ways
I praise God through each night.
For rhyme and rhythm I shall not own
All that comes from God
And draws His saving, sacred tunes
Upon Golgotha's rod.

God's Biblical text we humans read
Doth hold those truths of old
And all the promises He hath proclaimed
Shall save man's worldly soul.
For God, Great God, hath loved us so
To speak to every heart
Through fools like me in endless rhyme
To word His every part!

Earth's days hath drawn upon all time
Their fleeting, temporal sighs
And all those centuries come and gone
Hath all held ones like I.
For God doth use those talents fair
Of His creation—man,
And give them peace throughout their worth
To tell men of His stand.

As I draw end to my meek rhyme
Which scarce I hath not named
Should I call it love of heart?
Or creation's timeless reign?
I think this night upon my knees
I shall write His line
And call it God! Great God up high!
And praise Him through all time!

The everlasting space in which we berth
And light-years beyond the way
And creation's endless, timeless quest
Of God's great saving way.
For all those rhymes we pen in part
And all those lyrics ceased
Shall sing before the Son of Man
With love and Christ at peace!

GOD IN EACH AND EVERY PLACE
(And, Of Course, His Poets)

I know there're places far our there
Beyond the ocean's distant edge
Where skies are full of clouds and birds
And mountains rise and men do tread;
Where God hath blessed this bountiful earth
With all its foreign different songs,
Each drawing on God's giving hand,
Each one to Him we all belong.

I know there're cities tall and grand
Where thousands part their paths so wide
And men who stir the waves of time
And those who reach up for God's sky.
But we in all our biding lines
Doth toil and dream and earn our wage,
And put God's world upon our song
And rhyme His stars and word our page.

I hear there're nobles wrought with gold
And kingdoms blessed with armies strong,
And milk and honey beyond the measure
And beautiful women with loving songs.
But we in all our humble worth
Doth spread those thoughts of scholars far
And dream of countries filled to brim
Of distant skies and oceans' bars.

Alas, I know there're valleys green
Where clover grows and fountains flow,
Where children play and old men sup
And God eternal loves us so.
But poets in their foolish ways
Doth "while" their time which endless moves
Upon God's sacred forever stage
Of men and poets and amazing muse.

As we reach out to grasp thy wind
Which came afar from distant shore,
Those rhythms of some dearer songs
Guide our pens through pages tore;
And shan't the idle command our writ
All time eternal tis at its rage.
We dream of seashores wrought with those
Who live afar in ripeful age.

I know there's God who reigns up high
Upon His timeless eternal throne,
Where Christ doth hold the hands of those
Who kept His truths and sung His songs.
But, alas, our heart doth long for home
Of those who kept Christ's righteous score.
We dream of cities in His sky
With angels' love beyond God's door.

The night tis dark upon man's face
And freezing winds doth chill his soul,
And the morrow brings what it shall may
For God hath drawn His judgement scroll.
His love for us a 'flames the rhyme
And brings those lands upon our hearts
To teach and tell those long lost men
Of God and Jesus and new found starts.

His mission granted tis the one
Not from some foolish poet's mind,
But straight from out God's generous heart
For each and every wonderous kind.
To us He throws His challenged bid
Of rhyme and rhythm and sacred songs
To tell His world of forever birth
Of Christ and peace and loving home.

Yes, I know there're places for out there
Beyond God's oceans' distant edge
Where skies are full of clouds and birds
And mountains rise and men do tread.
Where poets toil with rhymes of old
And where Christ puts His rightful grace
Beside those distant lands in time
To each and all and every place!!!

GOD'S GREAT WORK

Through night eternal upon God's star
And lights born old in time
And millions and billions of endless years
And all God's loving rhymes.
They all t'wer given by God above
They all are His great works
And as we verse each passing page
We see God on this earth!

The snow-capped mountains above the plain
And skies of crystal blue
And depths of water upon the seas
Tell all that God tis true.
For each and every one of us
God penned in sacred rhyme
Hath all His wonderous works to view
Throughout our passing time!

Ages from out man's distant lore
Whence scholars impendent doth read
And all man's volumes of past gone text
Leave us in spiritual need.
God's all, God's great, His Biblical word
Shall endure throughout each age
And come right back to haunt those souls
Who reject all what God hath made!

The infinite pen God draws in time
Shall find its solace fair
And all His children God claimed on earth
Shall one day rise in air.
For above those hills of distant past
Shall come an angel's blare
A sound from out the sacred songs
Of Gabriel in the air!

The planets in their perspective place
And all earth's devious haste
All shall tremble by the hand
Of God's own righteous grace.
And those who knew His truths indeed
But never sought His love
They shall one day pass from time
Forever!   From above!

The awesome lights upon the skies
And systems of forever space
An eternal time from out God's void
Where no man hath ever graced
Brings us in every rhyme we make
To know our Lord tis grand
He gave us all His lovingness
And sowed the seeds of man!

Earth's passing time tis in a blitz
And rhymes are rolling on
From out Christ's eternal, hallowed writ
By loving, sacred songs.
For mortal men we are in lay
Hath scarce to hold the glass
To drink God's grandest eternal love
From out His blessed past!

The awesome heavens in their right
And stars upon God's skies
And forever grace He gave to us
Shows all, Christ loves us nigh.
He gave to all His blessings
And loves us every one
From out His eternal, lasting time
Till all His works are done!!!

GOD'S SACRED SPRING

In artist form God gave His land
His heart and endless love
He painted earth's rightful, awesome time
With spring!—And heaven above.
By whence the beauty God hath proclaimed
T'was given in His great joy
He held His hand and made each man
And rightly did deploy!

God's sacred spring t'was given in peace
Under some starry sky
Where dewdrops fall upon His stars
And angels never die.
God shook the mighty depths of time
And bent a moonbeam true
And fashioned this old earth with His spring
Just for me and you!

As poets pen throughout earth's days
And scent tis in God's air
Of spring and beauty and endless life
Bequeath to end despair.
Our Lord hath made the forest green
And bathed this world with love;
He even gave us wind that sings
From His great home above!

The beauty of the radiant fields
Shows each of us new life
And deer and squirrels and little ones
Adorn our earth this night.
For as some poet pens his love
To each new breath of spring,
Gabriel shall rightly send his song
From out great God, our King!

This fool who draws what tears he wept
Tis only but a serf
God uses in His rapturous love
To show this world His worth.
And as the years doth pass away
Another takes God's pen
And colors all this beautiful art
Intend for earthly men!

As Christ did bear the cross and death
His Father gave us, too,
His spring with all its dogwoods fair
And brand new life so true.
For as we mortals feel God's love
In spring with blossoms scent
Our Lord hath left that grave of old
And reigns in firmament!

Each spring we pick God's flowers lush
And place them in a vase
As if their beauty right proclaimed
Shall live throughout our race.
But as the petals turn away
From beauty God hath sent
We sorrow in the rue of scenes
And long for just intent!

As this poor soul doth end his rhyme
Of spring in God's own flair,
I wonder if those times of old
T'wer blessed by nature's care.
And as we draw our souls towards Him
And place Him in our hearts,
God shall rightly give us spring
That never will depart!

Yes, God doth give and God doth take
His seasons through the years
And dips his brush of many colors
Into earth's hopes and fears
And bathes this land which He proclaimed
With spring and beautiful life
And draw those things from out His heart
And place us in His sight!!!

GOD'S SUMMERTIME

Hotter as the wind, it blows into your face
Lighter than the air, you look and find your place.

Free as a lark, you transverse sand and sea
Caring what the good times hold made for you and me.

Visions of grandeur, you hold thou head up high
Daring what the deep water has to offer by and by.

Cooking out, that's fun, season from the earth
That's what times are for, valuable and worth.

Fishing from the hole, barefoot boy and breeze
Cricket on the line, waiting to be teased.

Dusty roads are calling graced with adventure show
Time to travel now and shun the winter's woe.

Warm nights and love tell oh Cupid's nigh
Waiting to slip in and start thou heart to cry.

Magnificent as the sky that tells of good times' fun
Fall will come abeckoning and put old summer on the run.

For God hath made it all, both land, sky and sea
Atonement for all his flock, just for you and me!

HERE TODAY AND GONE TOMORROW

As here today and gone tomorrow
Are each small drops of rain.
As eagles soar above the plain
They, too, shall pass the same.
And aging poets are not exempt
From falling from the rhyme.
Just here today and gone tomorrow
Are each and every kind!

The riches we seek from out this earth
Are but here for the hour,
And the palace we dream of in our dreams
Allude our human powers.
Each just and righteous deed we wrought
Entrenched into our hearts
Are here in soul and chamber's mold
And soon they shall depart!

Those buildings high above man's works
Shall one day fade from sight,
And the coin with which we pay our way
Tis here and gone tonight.
And those chores with which we toiled and rued
Shall one day hence be gone—
Just here today and gone tomorrow
Tis time's eternal song!

Earth's kingdoms grand in stately lands
Are follies on their way,
And the might which mighty armies bore
Are defeated by the day.
And the scarlet cloth which adorned the head
Of some lassie in the spring
Shall find its mark upon time's soil
And never will be seen!

Those foolish poets such as I
Who rhyme into God's night
And all their beautiful prolific thoughts
Shall never survive the blights.
And the gracious smile with which some gave
Are but a moment's thing.
All land and sea and you and me
Shall one day fade the scene!

As I in all my follies haste
Doth sit here by the light,
I rhyme in heart and search my soul
For each new thought to write.
For the grandest one who bore the rod
Shall pull my heart along
Into His forever eternal land
Where nothing shall be gone!

His kingdom in its glorious stance
Tis far from earth's ole turf,
And the lasting love with which He bore
Tis all eternity's worth.
Each gemstone casts upon this land
Shall never find its rank,
All that last tis what we give
And put in God's own bank!

As dawn draws forth from out earth's crest
And fowls soar in time's sky,
I raise my eyes upon some plain
And thank great God up high.
For all that last tis not the past
Nor what the earth shall bring.
All that lasts is our souls
And Jesus Christ our King!!!

KNOW THAT I AM GOD

As the sun rose above the meadows
And Earth's mankind took his place
Beside the annuals of time
In each sacred, hallowed space,
A crisp, deep blue, serene sky
Bordered the time-worn sod
While angels from the heavens
Sung, Thou art thy God.

Yea, man in his hour of plight and scorn
And the deeds he wrought upon this Earth
Seem to sadden the heart of him
Who pulled the Earth into his worth.
For as the days though cruel they seem
Convene the lives though right and odd,
Some angels in the highest realm
Declare to heaven that all tis God.

The streets of York are filled with men
Each striving to find their slots in life,
And shops are stocked with wares of them
Who barter with souls throughout the night
But time has reckoned its rightful hold
Upon man's brows each marked with age.
Our God sings out above the crowd
Be still and know and calm thy rage.

Earth's mountains rise into the skies
And centuries troubled with strifes of old,
Each country bound with shield and sword
And preachers preaching to hearts and souls.
These are the things which wax with age
Of man's encompasses throughout his toils.
But, yea, there tis a glory realm
Above the muck and from the spoils.

As tyrants in their splendid castles
Wrought death upon this saddened Earth
And the pillage and human misery
And the blood and death and hurt
There stands a force, eternal and true
So might with no pronounced defeat
That drags man's evil, sinful blights
Unto God's rightful, judgement seat.

The charge, though, swift as lightning bold,
And the trumpet's blareful, final sound
And legions of herald angels high
Shall converge upon some earthly town
And pluck the thorn from out their eyes
Of passionate men who kept God's faith
And send to those who lust in sins
Unto a final, horrible faith.

As poets such with this fool's pen
Draw the lines of centuries old
Of purpose, life, and all the rest
Of reason to live and seek a goal.
There lies procured upon some page
The words of Him who triumphed the rod
Wax truthful in thy worldly deeds
Be still and know that I am God.

The stars which shine God's glory high
And His untouchable, endless, timeless space
And the bodies so very far, far apart
That never will grace or see man's face.
So given by Christ the greatest God
And, too, with His approving
Come enter my heavenly final place
And know that I am truly God!

LIFE'S PONDEROUS

Adorn with life this whirling earth
Transverses God's timeless seas
By which it came, by which it goes,
Tis all creation's glee.
As vines of grapes from heaven grow
Throughout time's wonderous scene
Christ's fruits shall feed the souls of all
Who call Him Blessed King!

The shadows of earth's deepest dark
Hath scarce to dim God's light
For from out His boundless, timeless toil
Are rays of hope this night.
And from a wording fool as me
Are rhymes cast out to man—
They are the product of the One
Who gave us pen in hand!

As days that come are fleeting on
And tears invade our souls
Our grandest, eternal, awesome one
Hath scarce to leave his fold.
For by His grace with great exalt
Our Christ hath held His hand
Upon our bosom's tenderness
And gave His love to man!

The depths upon our furrowed brows
Doth show the scars of life
But all creation's, timeless works
Hath shown Our Maker's might.
For as some men deny the One
Who brought them earthly days,
Their writ in heaven's grading books
Shall be their eternal wage!

The words doth flow from out man's tongues
As they compete for life
Through earth's infernal, awesome quests
As poets toil this night.
For as the sparrow flies away
Shall all men take its heed
And look up to God's infinite sky
And grasp heaven's golden keys!

A foolish scribe as this poor slave
Who pens through dark of night
By earth's old hedious, uncertain berth
Hath seen God's saving light.
For every man before God's all
Shall one day pass away
Into God's endless forever verse
And give their lives away.

God's starlit heavens in awesome trance
Shall leave their place in time
And all those grandest works we penned
Shall pass away from rhyme.
For as this poet hath drawn his wage
Shall all this earth to be
A passing shadow upon the lines
Throughout all eternity.

For, from out the night with moonlite quest
Are rays of lights of old
While angels in their rightful stance
Are drawing our works to scroll.
For what we do and what we say
Doth be time's great intent
To send us on our eternal ways
Through hell or heaven sent!

LIFE'S SEARCHING

Life tis like the scholar
Searching far out some quest
Through miles and miles of faded dreams
From birth to growth to death.
And we, the children of our time,
Doth amplify our own
And speed our souls along that path
Where tread past men far gone!

Life tis like some summer
All filled with joys and hope
And beyond there lies a rainbow
As if our Lord hath spoke.
For life tis full of goodness
And if we searched in vain
We can find life's answer
All written in God's own name!

Life tis as some sparrow
Flying high and free
O'r a beautiful forest
By some tranquil sea.
For life tis not allusive
We each can grasp its hold
From out time's endless beauty
And place it in our souls!

Life tis of some dreamland
Where elves and angels trod
Away from all those sorrows
Which grip us as we plod.
For if we grasp its fleeting
Rays of warming love,
We shall find our dreamland
Sent straight from God above!

As we search in awesome
Lands, we know not where
Our paths hath crossed some meadow
Where no one hath forth dared.
For, lo! We see our journey
Hath run our trip to end
And climbed up to God's staircase
Right where we'd hoped it'd end!

From days all full of laughter
To sorrow by some grave
From daisies lush in blossoms
To painful, tireful days,
We each shall find our birthright
Carved with God's own great care
Upon His glorious bosom
For each one that He beared!

As fools doth pen their sonnets
Upon time's endless throne
There by some dim-lit cottage
Enhanced by word and song,
Our lives shall find their blessings
For each small work we rued
Upon that endless blue sky
From out eternity's truths!

As God doth give His searching
Children in all their pain,
He parts His timeless star seas
And loves each one the same
And brings life's endless searching
To each of us in truth
From out eternity's message
By heaven or hell conclude!

LIFE'S SITUATION

Alone we reap what harvest grew
From out our tear-soaked cries
And draw to soul what we hath gold
God's great, eternal skies.
We humans fetch our wares unto
Life's fleeting marketplace
And sell those things which we hath clinged
Throughout our turbulent pace!

As mortal men upon this earth
We strike our deals in gold
And garner what we can from life
To save our allusive souls.
For little do our thoughts hath quest
Before God's greatest sighs
We sadden His loving bliss at best
And deny our Saving Sire!

As doubting upon this whirling ball
Hung in God's firmament mist
We scourge the very tender heart
Of Christ's own lovingness.
We men of Rome hath cast aside
What grave our God hath shown
And think that all the wealth and jewels
Will save our tottering own!

We save unto life's vast own plan
Our wailing, selfish worths
And perplex the very heart of Him
Who gave us life at birth.
For as the rushing seasons pass
Our eyes so full of "own",
Our souls t'wer poorer by the hand
Of time's own imminent loan!

We village slaves with all our quest
Hath scarce to read the hour
For least we shall now know unto
Our God shall claim His power
And reap those blessings right upon
His sheep and cast away
This balmy earth with sinning surfs
And send His judgement day!

We sit here by our candle's lights
And "pen" our souls along
Upon time's eternal, endless flights
Unto a sea of "own."
And place our values high unto
Our graven, gold-like trance
And dream of all those things we deed
Into our worldly stance!

As mortals we are called unto
The breath and sight of life
And given each we passing few
Who praise God's holy might,
Those keys which hold the depth from us
And bring our hearts to bear
Unto God's heavenly, blessful grace
To righten and to fair!

As deathly haste doth quence our life
And man hath laid to waste
God's endless, forever, loving light
Upon time's eternal pace
We Christians hath but sure to draw
Those things which gave us love
And cling to treasures beyond this flesh
From somewhere high above!

As I draw end to my small writ
Upon time's endless skies
And pen what hath God dared to bind
Into my book of cries,
I scarce hath seed my lyrics' songs
In soils of earthly past
Before the Great Jehovah One
Hath drained my hourglass!

With life and birth and beautiful nights
Earth's men doth draw their greed
Up to God's loving, generous heart
In downright pious deeds.
Men cast and scorn God's infinite love
Unto their selfishness
And charge their souls throughout their roles
Unto the eternal quest!!!

LOVE AND PURPOSE

This starry night above our heads
And depths no one can see
And trails of tears through light-years filled
And oceans of ebony seas.
All t'wer made by God on high
Since creation's blissful song
And all t'wer given in hallowed love
To fill our hearts that long!

The infinite skies with soaring fowl
And clouds that adorn this land
And seas with currents no man can tread
Except the Son of man.
For all t'wer put here not by chance
All t'wer given in love
From time eternal through eons spent
All from God above!

The sobering toils we humans face
Are not the end of time
And all those heartaches by the way
Are not our final rhymes.
For God, Great God, hath loved us so
He brought us life and breath
And paved the way for eternal days
And gave us righteous wealth!

The mountains' peaks thrust towards the sky
And valleys are emerald green
And forest so thick before our eyes
For all doth show our King
Since time eternal t'was forth bequeathed
And we t'wer made by grace
Our God hath given us endless life
And set us in our place!

Our voluminous texts we humans read
Throughout our short-spaced days
Are mortal man's attempt of why??
We humans scribe our rage
And pace and ponder each abstract line
To whence we come from where??
Can not we see in sacred love
We came by God's own care!

Our longing hearts doth gaze the skies
To see what we can see
All time eternal before our face
And life around like we.
But as we look upon our earth
We see God's marvelous signs
The wealth He gave us time again
And brought us endless rhymes!

As poets draw their hearts to bear
And tears flow from each page
The Greatest One from out all time
Doth guide us through each age
And show us what new peace we have
If only we take the charge
And lay our hearts before His throne
And love Him by and large!

The infinite time no man hath seen
Stretches away to space
And love eternal though by God's hand
Doth move to some new place.
We humans reach out for the one
Who gave us lasting wealth
And loved us in our frailing rhymes
AND SAVED US BY HIS DEATH!!!

LOVE NOTES

Love notes, love notes
We weave in endless rhyme
Throughout this vast, aging earth
And word each passing line.
For each and every love note
We pen in every part,
We draw upon the arrow
Of Cupid's loving heart!

Love notes, love notes
For whence the passion strikes
Upon some moonlite meeting
Of two hearts in some night.
For all the earthly treasure
Shan't buy the gift from God
And play our beautiful love notes
Straight from the arrow's rod!

Love notes, love notes
Alone and one at last
For all time's beautiful love notes
Hold all God made that last
And pull our lives together
Upon God's misty sea
Through time's own just intentions
From out God's blessings free!

Love notes, love notes
For whence they play His song.
God's grandest, wonderful melodies
From out the days so long.
And draw His timely rhythms
Upon our needing hearts
And play God's beautiful love notes
From out His boundless art!

Love notes, love notes
For joys through time that last
And cause God's flowing fountain
To fill our loving glass
To drink from out His blessings
And pledge our hearts so true
And sing His grander melodies
Till heaven and earth are two!

Love notes, love notes
The night tis cold and dark
And rhythms flow from memories
From out our aging hearts.
For fairer tis the morning
With all its passionate dew
To cover our beautiful love notes
Till time comes forth anew!

Love notes, love notes
The years pass long at last.
They hold those bountiful memories
Of two, in time, that passed
And traveled up God's staircase
To Christ and loving home
Together with their love notes
Forever! In their song!

Love notes, love notes
All time in all its worth
Shan't equal one little heart trob
From out God's beautiful earth.
For all the endless pleasure
His two have on their own
Tis all the grandest treasure
Of lovers in their home!

Love notes, love notes
Through time's own endless reign
From moonbeams upon some meadow
From out all endless fame.
For fairer tis God's love notes
We draw on passionate scroll
And sign our names to heaven
Throughout time's centuries old!

Love notes, love notes
They play on cherry hearts
This night upon our blessings
With yearning, striving parts
And spew forth songs of fairer
Days and years ahead
And cause God's beautiful love notes
To go right to our heads!

Love notes, love notes
For whence we sing anew?
From out God's endless blessings
And for two hearts so true?
For mighty tis God's power
Upon His sacred throne
He holds the lines to love notes
Throughout the years all gone!

Love notes, love notes
The hour tis late at hand
For writing beautiful love notes
Doth move the rhyme that ran
And bring us one, together,
Upon God's greatest own
From out His beautiful love notes
To Jesus, on and on... .

MARVELOUS

This changing world in which we live
Tis all the gift from God
For upon His eternal, noble work
He sowed us in His sod.
And rightful, hence, He made the air
And all those things within
To show us with His generous heart
What love He hath intend!

The ocean's roar upon some beach
In never-ceasing stride
And all the life God chose to place
Into His water's tide
Doth give to us a sense of love
Of what our Master drew
From out His timeless, eternal work
Just for me and you!

The eternal nights with starry sky
Upon a sea of time
And stars that shine throughout God's void
In never-ending rhyme
Brings all we humans before His throne
To see what God hath made.
He even gave His forest trees
And placed us in their shade!

He caused the hills before His sky
To rise amid this earth
And christened all the meadows fair
And gave them green and worth.
For God hath placed His hand upon
Our lives in such a way
He even gave us eternity
With all its serious lay!

The temporal bond which each we hold
Upon this planet earth
Shall one day pass upon that scene
Of angels in their berth
And bring our lives and souls to rest
By whence He placed the sky
For all His children by their worth
And dried our crying eyes!

He blesses all who seek His love
Amid man's evil scene
And pardons all who wish to seek
Our never-ending King.
For by our souls we hold the fee
Which someday tis our own
To turn the lock on heaven's doors
And walk up to God's throne!

We humans shall upon that time
Draw all our treasures nigh
To whence we dealt our earthly chores
And loved His Son up high.
For by each day we lived in tune
With God's own righteous band
We shall play in grandest form
His harp with heavenly clan!

Time's starry lights as jewels upon
Earth's deepest, darkest place
Doth show our souls for what God made
And saved us by His grace.
For only Christ upon our hearts
Shall bring our final rhyme
Into God's greatest, eternal house
FOREVER! THROUGH ALL TIME!!!

MY SONG OF INSPIRATION
(In the Morning)

It is but six in the morning
The sun hath just stroked earth's leaves—
A robin, faint, sings from some bushes
And all the fields have their seed—
For—a scurry, ole creature like me
One who grapples with life and the pen—
A radiance shines warm in my soul
As God and the heavens trip in!

What a choir to chorus my day,
What an anthem to lighten my dark—
The little small notes of the rhyme
Arranged in an orchestrated bark!
But—oh, for a small, hushed sonnet
One which vibrates the strings of some heart
And echoes the wind of a new morn
As tho sung from a dramatized harp!

One which pours the honey from the beehive
And covers my lines with some cream—
So all the rhythms come out
Like roses and fragrances and things!
While all earth's living come forth-with
As tho from an eternal sleep
And wipe the dew from their wood-paths
And rejoice in a heavenly peace!

A tune of the "Rock of Ages"
Some gift to this poet of old
A sonnet which rightens the wrong deed—
And soothes the fresh-born doe
And all the lyrics fall harmony
Which God hath deemed as tho—
An acorn t'was given in blessing
To a little cold squirrel in the snow!

There's something great in this hour and moment
There's power of the rhyme in the air—
Oh, God—why sparest this sin-slave
Who writes with tricks of a flair?
You could mow this creature, a meddling
Into the pit he's dug for all time
And never once silence your anthem
Which governs the songs of all rhyme!

I gaze at earth's far horizon,
I sense something great with awe
Just humming my tune in the morning
Tis all I could do or could know—
Oh, God, He's great with His blessings;
A fool, such as me can well tell;
But, oh, for that rhyme in the morning
The inspiration which bids my day well!!!

NO GUARANTEE

Life tis a very precarious thing
So seemingly I've been told
And many who tread these roads of earth
Grow weary, tired and old.
For each and every tear we shed
Shall somehow flow our pain
Into life's eternal, endless nights
Of heartache whenced with blame!

It matters if ye grieve a lot
And shun those works of old
Those words which bring our souls to bear
Upon God's eternal scrolls.
The rains shall fall, the winds shall blow
And never will call back
Tomorrow with its impetuous rue
By poets' lack for fact!

Time's meadows wrought with daisies' breath
And the little, small bees of life
Each one hath graced its place it seems
And vanished into God's night.
A chill of wind from out the north
Doth cool those fires we flamed
And erased our brief-like tracks we wore
Upon God's endless plain!

The soft, scented couch of death and grief
Haunts us by the hour
And venomous follies so sad and bleak
Shall triumph o'r our own powers.
We came here free of debt and sin
But shant our lives right sever.
We now are broke and bear the yoke
Before the great forever!

This life tis full of plites and vice
From out time's cruel, old spanned
And throughout those eons past and bleak
Comes devoirous deeds enhanced.
As poets such as this fool's soul
Doth scribble into God's night,
The moving pen hath scribed the lines
Of harrowing, horrendous sights!

What matter if the walls of time
Do cave in and give way
And cover our little paths we took
Along God's Milky Way??
The infinite sky hath seen it all
From birth, cradle and grave—
Of each and every word we spoke
Upon time's endless age!

As blunders of the chosen few
Hath sealed their doomed-like faiths,
We slaves of time and endless rhyme
Doth word in all our haste.
As sure as Moses struck with "staff"
And Adam sinned with Eve,
We grieve God's heart throb worlds apart
And succumb with disbelief!

Earth's nights promise none of scent and myrrh
And life hath no guarantee
Of happy times all filled with goods
Content with peace so free.
For as these words hath claimed the page
Of voluminous texts of man,
We trip and stumble throughout our age
And speed the hour hand!

The eternal oceans do beat our shores
And God's skies are endless seas
Upon time's great, horrendous stage
Wrought with you and me.
For all we have tis what we give
In each and every passing
And pay the toll and hope God's scroll
Has us for our asking!!!

NAZARETH

The worth of Earth's great banks
The primest sheep of the fold
The highest level obtained
And a pure possessor of soul.
All have very high marks
And all have limits once set.
But, oh, for that Nazareth place
Where man and his Maker once met.

The humblest of all Earth's creatures,
The summum bonum of life;
The nave and the fairest of damsels
And the king and his beautiful wife
All have very good qualities
And all have courage and might.
But, oh, for that Nazareth place
Long ago on a star-filled night.

The highest ranking of soldier
The strongest man of Earth
The wisest teacher of humanity
And the smell of a perfume's myrrh
All have a passionate worth,
And all are sought by man.
But, oh, for that Nazareth place
The cradle of God's wonderful plan.

ORDAINED MISSION

From out this time of aging rhyme
My God hath called to me
His forlorn, striving, penning slave
To draw His love to be.
And move time's ink and scribe forthwith
Into some sacred verse
From out God's boundless, endless love
And pen His heart to earth!

This hallowed rhyme upon earth's page
Hath all seen war and strife
And drawn those lyrics through eons spent
Into some turbulent night
And sped the Christ Child's love into
The very heart of man
From sacred words to saving worth
God's writ hath born a plan!

As Potter and His clay t'was spent
To give forth from this earth
A beautiful vessel made by man
And show the Maker's work
For so tis of some poet's rhyme
It is what is to be
A moving, ensuing thought to bear
Upon time's endless sea!

This poet hath but gone away
To counsel with the night
And ask what merry thoughts to bear
And what is there to write??
Alone and softly whispered hence,
Some voice shall come to me
Tis of some far grander plan
Than I can worldly see!

William Furr

The "cock" crows twice upon God's work
And brings me to respond
And hurled those truths upon time's page
From God's outstretching arms
And pull together loving verse
And call the stars to be
A halo for the Sacred One
Who died on Calvary!

As pen and slave doth move along
This shan't disturb God's "myrrh"
Shed along time's forever role
And bathed this hallowed earth.
God's stardust hath but cleansed a path
Up to that road so high
And anointed all who claim His name
Christians! By and by!

The boundless toil of each lost soul
Hath all but fallen way
Into time's eternal, forever mix
Of devils and their prey.
For God hath pulled His sacred ones
From harm and drudgery
And made their hearts a hallowed part
Through all eternity!

This moving pen I hold in grasp
Tis a chosen right
With God Almighty at the helm
From stardust through the night
And born His love from out time's past
Of grander rhymes so true
Of Jesus and His blessed ones
Through heaven straight to you!!!

OUR GREAT GOD

T'was spring upon the cool, wet morn
And Earth had awoke amid the new dawn
For high in the skies all above the land
T'wer angels a'singing heaven's jubilant songs.
The cross lay barren all stripped of its use
And a dark, cold tomb lay empty and hushed.
God's world had hosted His Prince-of-a-Son
Who bore the sins, the ravages, of Earth.

Oh, God, thy lilies which rise from the fields
And the little, soft petals of life thy hath sprung
Shan't match thy glory of all of your skies
Where Christ, our Savior, did triumphantly come.
His presence among the throngs of this Earth
T'was given by Thee from heaven above.
His face shines bright upon this fresh spring;
His heart tis pure as sanctified love.

The summer drew nigh with fields, oh, so full
And forests grew lush into God's blue skies,
For barefoot boys t'wer playing their games
For this t'was a time to love and to sigh.
But, amid all the clamor of men and their own
There stands a keeper of Earth and its mirth,
For Jesus, our Lord, hath moved His great hand
And caused the heavens to give us our berth.

Oh, God, thy greatest, which governs the land
And, love eternal which beholds the frail eye
Shall live throughout the rapture of souls
And reside into the brilliant night sky.
Thy gift thy givest t'was bought with the rod
And blood thy paid t'was food for our souls.
For we in all our human requests
Hath scarce to grasp their ecumenical goals.

Then fall drew soft upon this world's face
And timid little animals played in the breeze.
For the cool of the wind cleansed God's fields
While poets, such as I, penned to the leaves
As autumn exploded in all grand array
And those colors a'glow painted His land.
The power of Him, so mighty and great
Admonished Earth's sins while the hourglass ran.

Oh, God, thy Keeper of the truth and the just
Thy presence doth humble the profits of man.
Thy love tis claimed by the greatest and least
Thy word tis read by the tongues of this land.
Oh, give us Your courage and casts us Thy truth
To never relinquish thy grip on our souls.
Give us the lyrics to the harps of Your stars
And rhyme Earth's seas and save all our souls.

Ole winter crept in as a chill cooled the scene
And God t'was in power asserting His call.
By rapturous glory and eternal bliss
His message t'was read from every church hall.
For Christmas t'was here and spirits t'wer high,
And the Christ Child lay swaddled and resting in peace.
As Mary and Joseph knelt by the stall,
An angel appeared while Jesus did sleep.

As fools, such as I, pen through Earth's night
And spill their feelings, their love aches, their souls;
Of years, of tears, of eternal plites
Of beautiful places with streets of pure gold,
There stands amid the wonders of time
A picturesque season straight from God's heart
Bequeathed to all who peer from the page
And read the lines of His great loving art!!!

PLANTING

Upon life's rows we sow our seeds
And plow them into soil
For that which sprouts from out our works
Doth exemplify the toils.
For all we men of distant place
Hath shown our God at hand
With each and every sprout we raise
Upon time's eternal sand!

We humans in all our "pious lives"
Hath planted our seeds in time
From out God's mercy in our quest
And drawn on miles of rhyme.
For as we water each fragile seed
And cultivate the rows
Our rhythms shall sprout from out our toils
By what our harvest grows!

As weeks shall pass upon our crops
And if we watered fair,
There shall rise God's grandest hopes
To feed our souls each care.
For all those little weeds we pulled
Along life's jungle sage
Shall bring to light an amazing sight
Of fruits upon God's age!

Those "stalks" born true from out God's work
Hath glorified His stand
To bring to earth His saving worth
And free the hearts of man.
For as we humans prune away
At time's own growing crops
We scarce to see the fruits to be
From out God's eternal plot!

We go to town to buy our seed
And plan our every rows
And grow some beautiful flowers, too,
To amplify what shows.
For God Almighty hath given us work
His great and just intent
To born those labors with whence we toil
From out time's firmament!

As we "beam" on what we grow
We long for cooler days
Intune with nature's, wonderous pride
To glorify God's ways.
For as we harvest what God hath done
We till time's fertile land
And sow more seeds of righteous deeds
Throughout God's fall at hand!

God's harvest grows throughout our sweat
And hungry mouths are fed
Through sacred, caring, loving works
While God hath justly said,
"My fruits are for the endless reigns
Each child of Mine shall use
To feed those souls in glorious roles
Throughout all time infused!"

The land tis quiet through winter's wake
And snow tis right at hand
And all those toils throughout our while
Hath raised the hopes of man.
For as we look up to that scene
The harvest of God's souls
Our efforts spent sent many lives
Into God's grandest roll!!!

POET GONE

As we stand in awe and contemplate
We a'front a spectacular sea
Of eternal, endless, beautiful lights
Given by God to see.
For from this land we earthlings hold
Those truths which make us strong
Of God Almighty residing where
His angels sing His songs!

As we wax upon our faiths
And trauma confronts our days
As time and place and strenuous pace
Doth speed the poets' lays
We stare and gaze and are amazed
At starry lights and sky
Of God, Great God, residing where
Our sonnets are to lie!

We humans in our pitiful works
Doth charge the soul at best
And divergent pace and worldly grace
Doth hurt the heart's own quest.
For as the sands of endless rhyme
Confront our spirit's song
We tottle upon this rock called earth
And speed our souls along!

Earth's truths we hold close to our hearts
Are but the hour present
And looming over our fainting rhymes
Stretches the great forever.
For as the sands of moving time
Hath scribbled the sonnet's rage
We stumble in our frail-like ways
And flounder in our days!

As kingdoms rise upon some land
With armies right engage,
Confront our every trembling hearts
And turn our tear-soaked page.
We humans in our ambivalent quest
Hath scarce to save our rhyme
From out this blasphemous, pitiful earth
And stop the hands of time!

Perplexed are we in daily works
From whence we hath gone wrong
And strike the staff upon some rock
And bid the hour gone.
We sadden the generous heart of Him
Who gave us new-found days
And turn the pages of passing rhyme
And draw on earthly wage!

As I confront these worldly words
Which come into my rhyme
And think of Great Jehovah One
Who gave us our own kind
And of a power so right and true
From out God's striving best
I fall down on my knees and cry
Oh, God! Give us Thy rest!

Some say time's moving ambivalent signs
Charge wherein they stand
To scholars of the greatest minds
To record our words that ran.
But, oh, the greatest rhyme we knew
Doth lie within His heart
Our Christ Almighty residing where
We poets have embarked!!!

REDEMPTION
(Of Choice)

Far away in distant time
Beyond an ocean of depth and sea
Over enchanted starlit sights
And from the miles our eyes can see
Came forth our God in all His might
And took those reins of sky and space
And made His choice upon this earth
To grant each child His loving grace!

Those endless, vibrant, love-struck nights
Which hold our hearts and grip our souls
Doth draw we earthlings to His might
From time eternal to endless roles
And born His children with His great plan
Thus granted upon earth's skies and seas
From out that darkness cold and still
God gave each one his right to be!

The mortal thoughts we scholars write
Which come forth from our tear-stained hearts
And all those allusive thoughts we dared
Have no place in creation's art.
For God Almighty hath moved His hand
And given the stars their endless range
And born from out His boundless depths
Our hopes, our dreams, in love proclaimed!

Time's endless miles we humans tread
And wear our "paths" upon God's heart
And dare to look back at our lives
And see our works in peace and part.
We hold the keys to endless grace
Less we in all our follies lose
That privilege to inflame those souls
And show what God hath chose to use!

Earth's sacred cows in offering place
And effigies of some worldly god
Still hold the hearts of foreign lands
Where men attest they know not God
For vipers in some scurry pit
Are fed those souls of past-gone lays
And precarious depths hold damned those ones
Whence gave their hearts to devious ways!

Earth's voluminous notes are scribed in stone
Upon each chilly, forlorn morn
And buzzards soar above some death
Where men abide with bodies torn.
For each small day that passed us by
Holds great the promise of redemptive love
For God Almighty hath swayed our nights
To day! To light! From heaven above!

Time's moving hand doth place our days
Into the morrow right or wrong
And loose the "leash" about our necks
And turn us loose to choose our home.
For Christ, the Perfect One, who gives
His humble children in their own birth
Those saving lines of "Amazing Grace"
If only we accept His worth!

The heavens swallow all who tread
Upon its bosom with their souls
And moves God's infinite, eternal plan
Out from its moorings, staunch and bold.
For God Almighty hath passed His rhyme
Unto we humans in disarray
And made His best upon this earth
For all who love and right obey!

As I, in closing, try to spell
What greatest love hath done for me
In all my blundering throughout the muck
God grants His sacred love for free.
For time eternal holds the keys
To front God's vast, everlasting space
And rhyme our lyrics by what dare
We give our souls in earthly place!

REFLECTIONS

From out a flame in timeless space
Our God hath moved His hand
And born what life He choose to make
And made us mortal man.
He hung His stars above our heads
And made the air and seas
To give us life and breath at large
And love us endlessly!

We mortal men of planet earth
Have all been charged with love
To spread creation's timeless tune
And praise God up above
And live each day with passing rhymes
To show our love at heart
And tell of Jesus endlessly
To save men in their dark!

We doubting ones caught up in grief
Should all reject earth's spoils
And turn our eyes towards God on high
And praise Him by our toils.
Each day that passes hath many seen
Our works and endless lays
We are the example of our Lord
So live it by each day!

A struggling poet, as I, at large
Hath scarce to word my rhyme
Before the greatest hour hand
Doth claim my fragile time.
For God shall send His ones for me
To close my writ and cease
And guide me to His golden throne
Before the Prince of Peace!

Those volumes that I scribed and raged
T'wer not the things that last
For all those lines I drew with heart
Are all in timely past.
Those things which God hath deemed as true
Are love and righteous worth
They are the saving, sacred tunes
That last throughout this earth!

The years upon my pen it seems
T'wer hard by human rhyme
And all those tears I shed along
Are not the end of time
For we, in all our toiling works,
Doth need Christ endlessly
To draw our rhythms upon those hearts
As Christ doth set men free!

The night doth end in but a while
And I am still at rhyme
Drawing love notes on each page
And praising my God in time.
For by my words I doth proclaim
What Christ hath done for me
And know that I am one of His
Throughout all eternity!

The skies are high above our earth
As men doth toil away
Before the Greatest One on High
Who loves us day by day.
For all our tunes we draw in time
Shall be the final gauge
Which God Almighty shall forth use
To judge us by each page!!!

REPLENISHING

Far, far from the absence of our earth
Time's endless rue of shore sand burns
As "breakers" roll in and pull out to their sea
And the balmy, deep ocean perpetuately churns.

Those "portals" from which we viewed in this life
Twer no less than our souls portrayed
Upon God's eternal never-ending "span"
Through void and matter and lives displayed.

Time's "bosom" bequeathed to man's frail toil
Tis surging past earth's "famine and feast"
While lust and greed doth "seal" the faith
Of tireless souls of devious feats.

The "meca" which looms from out man's sand
Tis but the "oasis" of impotent desire
God's truth and righteous and starlit nights
Doth pass our graves in all their attire.

As nations rise upon the crest
Of "glorious" cities with statues bold
Those "columns" which hold man's seemingly "fame"
Shall crumble as the days wax old.

This life tis but the rhythm of time
All in its boldest, starkest form—
What little we learn from our mistakes
Shall haunt us to eternity born.

As children play throughout the land
And old men prepare their eternal home,
Those heavens above man's aging "mess"
Look down with tears and frownful scorn.

Our God in control of His greatest plan
Knows all our minds and fearful hearts
Of each of us upon our "bloom"
From dawn to dawn and dark to dark.

As years pass swiftly upon our scene
And time hath taken its rightful toll,
The heart shall cry from out the man
Oh, God, please save our longing souls!"

Our Christ in all His splendorest ways
Doth both understand and love obeys,
For man has "waxed" his "polished box"
And slips both silently into his grave.

The wind blows cold from throughout the field
And "markers" place our "final stand"
Upon that earth that we called home
And sanctified God's "rhyming hand."

The world has all gone to the "infinite space"
And the void stretches across the endless deep—
What matter if some "wretch" twas spared?
Another one shall find his "beat"!!!

REWARD

There comes a second in every life
When body and soul must part;
There is in every bloom in spring
A beginning and a start—
If your labors are abrupt and short
Or lingering and very long,
For tomorrow "cheer" hence comes the bride
And leads us to our home!

He will take your hand, oh, my little one,
And part earth's waters wide
While mending the tottering heart so faint
And comforting those that cried.
Aside from the jewels of rulers and kings
Far, far from the bread and wine,
If poor be less their glory shall be
To sing with the angels in time!

SEARCHING

Allusive as the rainbow's gold
Upon some dreamer's futile plot
To rid this bountiful rich ripe land
And plunder all its treasures' lot.
The infinite chamber where rhymes are made
Hath all but cast and hurled away
Some wretched rhyme of fading lines
And scorn each passing newborn day!

The incongruous wealth with which men seek
Tis some poor soul's tainted toils
And all thy glistening, sparkling gems
Have all seen mankind winched and soiled
For he who searched and he who lurked
Into life's canyons beneath the sky
Shall find his treasure farther than
Some shattered dream before his eye!

The oceans pull from out its roll
And serene, blue sky with soaring fowl
And the depths of space upon time's face
Allude our grasp and leave dumbfound
Mankind, as we, in pitiful lay
Emboss our souls and scribe some stone
Which stretch along in endless rows
Before eternity's forever song.

Incensed with shame we blame some crowd
With all our failures by their scale
And strive to pull right to our hearts
Our "all supreme" to no avail.
We pace, we pout, and reason, thus
Why whence some goal doth us allude??
Tis not the rightful bliss of time
But merely ill-timed solitude!

Man's factions grasp for riches hence
And morn to dark we grope our way
Upon this life's cruel-spent domain
And lust for "that" which got away.
We scarce to reason by our souls
That this tis not God's treasurers sent
But only love and peace of heart
Tis God's righteous just intent!

We wax our songs from out our souls
And barter with our aging minds
And spent what little time we cleave
Unto God's eternal, forever rhyme.
Those riches whence we seek in vain
Tis but some allusive forlorn verse
The only thing that shall forth last
Tis God's righteous saving worth!

Those sacred fowls up in His sky
And millions of stars beyond this scene
And foolish poets who toil by night
Hath all exalted God's wonderous fling.
Man's aging rhymes of scribbling worth
Shall move away from riches sent
And draw those rhythms toward our hearts
Of God and Christ and wonderment!

That rod upon some rugged hill
And darkness on this battered earth
For Jesus Christ the Son of Him
Doth guide this pen for all this worth
And search and search in due respect
We poets with our thoughts intuned
Whence come our frailing hearts to say
We found God's love in sacred bloom!!!

SUMMATION

Through the dark of night this chastized earth
Hath drawn upon God's hand
And winched and grieved and spewed-forth that
Which gives us rhymes that ran.
For as God's sacred time of year
Doth began to shed its pain
We humans in our worldly ways
Reject God's wonderous fame!

Oh, we, the chosen, infelicitous ones
From out time's long-gone sighs
Hath toiled and rued upon this earth
And cast our pitiful cries
Into some chosen wind we threw
Our insidious, bilingual works
And drawn on what our worldly gold
Can barter and exert!

The busy pace throughout man's days
And precarious, insidious lies
And all time's lore except from that
Which tis God's loving sighs,
Tis but a passing writ of few
We humans in fatuous trance
From out time's moving, eternal feats
We never once hath glanced!

This poet true to men and scroll
Doth draw his rhymes to write
Upon time's infinite, undaunted quest
Until the morning's height
And moved his callous pen onto
Some sacred hallowed page—
Great God Almighty residing where
Our sonnets come of age!

The angels in God's heavenly place
Sit right beside His throne
And see our rhymes of mortal lay
And grade our text alone.
For whence we grieve on stringent lines
And voluminous script we wept
Great Gabriel in his power glance
Shall read the rhyme we left!

As years turn into centuries old
And we hath left this place
Upon which gave the grace to choose
The rhyme we set in place.
Our sonnets in their final hour
Twer cast into some sea
Years and years and tears ago
By likes of you and me!

God's heavens hold the future tense
Away from strifes of old
And fairer tis Christ's sacred love
Beyond this wrath and cold.
For as the years doth bide us by
And pens and paper cease
The rhymes we cast to God up high
Shall be our greatest feats!

Some say time's endless, wonderous signs
Twer given by the hand
Of God's own righteous saving love
To bless this earth and man.
And from His timeless forever writ
Which charges our last pen
We give the hallowed sacred Christ
Our keys to let Him in!!!

SWEETY
(for Little Jennifer)

Ah, Sweety tis a bird of sorts
A friendly wing of God;
He flutters through the minds of child
Where elves and angels trod.

This humble bird, so soft and kind
Should make little Jennifer's day,
For angels of the little ones
Respect the parakeet's way.

Now Sunshine died late that night
While little hearts swept the sky
In search of dreamland over the moon
to love, listen, and cry.

Oh, Sunshine's gone but Sweety's left
A single radiant bird
Shall bless the hearts of little girls
Through God's soft-spoken word!

UP AND OVER THE SUMMIT

Over the towering summit
We climb and pull ourselves
Where each we hath surmounted
Time's treacherous, perilous stairs.
For scaling up life's pinnacles
As we in time shall do
Tis God's own blissful rhyming
Of fleeting signs we view!

Over the looming peak
Whence few hath scaled alone
To God's right hand we reach out
And grasp His beautiful home.
Since time eternal tis blissful
For all who climb with God
There shall be the Christian
Who loved Christ on that rod!

As we pull upon boulders
Those dark, cold-like stones,
We reach out for the summit
And feel our way along.
But, yea, we find our crevice
In which to place our line
And pull our very beings
Up from God's sands of time!

Our God doth bring life's mountains
Unto our eyeful stay
Upon His ranging hilltops
To each He gave a way.
There by the precarious pathways
We humans shall climb forthwith
To find our sacred treasure
Tis is God's golden gift!

The journey tis a rough one
With each new rock we grasp
And precarious divers' places
Hold each our lives intact.
For treacherous, hideous pathways
That led to God's own throne
Are worth all climbing up there
For we are not alone!

Those impasses upon our climbing
Which impede and obstruct our aims
Are some way forthright manageable
To reach our Lord and gain
Heaven's beautiful city, blissful
In all its hallowed place,
Upon God's beautiful hilltop
Where each He gives His grace!

As we near God's summit
We see those golden stairs
Where no stone left tis waiting
To block us from His care.
We shrug off our last boulders
And place our feet on home
And run right up God's staircase
Forever in a song!

Life tis not a leisure
For each who walk with God
We must take charge of scaling
And timely, precariously plod
Up to God's grandest hilltop
Whence men hath sought so true
And leave this blasphemous earth
And find our home anew!!!

THE BEST THINGS OF THIS EARTH

As men cast lots upon a sea
In search of wealth and greed
As mankind invokes his evil plots
And mayhem runs so free.

The things that last and things that are
Those God-given gifts of worth
The sky! The wind! The cresting sea
Are the best things of this earth!!!

A looming sun draws forth its rays
And paints the land so green
And the ripen fields of corn and hay
Adorn our every scene.

The sky's so blue and the wind so high
And seas with pounding surf
These are gifts one cannot buy
The blest things of this earth!!!

The lush-filled valleys of bear and elk
And the call of the lark overhead
The thick green forest with deer and squirrel
And the desert with jewel-floor swept.

Those intricate gifts our Maker adorns
Are those that last in worth
These are the love God gave to us
The best things of this earth!!!

A deer stands tall with grace and pose
And little rabbits catch our sight
And rolling long plains tremble below
A thunder-filled sky with might.

The eternal seas pound timeless shores
And put our souls to berth
For the night draws endless, forever rhyme
The best things of this earth!!!

As poets cast forth their weary lots
And put their thoughts to rest
Upon God's forever endless time
Of love and joy and best.

Some breeze shall stir the cloud-filled skies
And turn our hearts toward mirth
Those scented, sweet forever rhymes
The best things of this earth!!!

As I end now my late night verse
Of what we have so free
Time, space, and that love between
This earth and all eternity.

My thoughts turn toward a richer gift
One that graced this earth
Jesus Christ and His love abound
Are the best things of this earth!!!

AMERICA, OUR HOME
(A song)

As far as the eye can see
We stand and awe the setting sun
Upon God's eternal land He gave
In love and joy with battles won.
We scarce to glimpse the standing buck
His proud pose with his antlers tall
Beneath us lies the cooling grass
Entangled wit the life that crawls.

Oh,--

America, America, our homeland of the free
Surround us with thy beauty fair
Keep us by thy seas.
Make us mindful of loving prayer
Give us time alone
Guard us in our every ways
FOR, AMERICA, WE SING YOUR SONG!!!
WE LOVE OUR AMERICA'S HOME!!!

Beside the lake with willow trees
By way of brook and running stream
There lies the love God gave in grace
For all who join His righteous team.
This country, this land, He gave in grace
Holds forth the beauty of our souls
It causes us to live with peace
For all who claim His honor roll.

Through wars and thick of battle lines
She draws her mark upon time's sand
And proudly gives all who seek
Her love, her all, her infinite plan.
Our country, our America, our home at large,
Tis what God gave for us to see
A joy, a beauty, a loving home
For all who seek her patiently.

By lamp, by fire, some cooling night
The flicker reflects her time-worn past
Of sacrifice and loving souls
Who gave their all so she could bask.
We shan't forget those tearful drops
Of men who gave their all for her
We must in our own living tense
Love and respect and thus concur.

America, America, our homeland of the free
Surround us with thy beauty fair
Keep us by thy seas
Make us mindful of loving prayer
Give us time alone
Guard us in our every ways
FOR, AMERICA, WE SING YOUR SONG
WE LOVE OUR AMERICA'S HOME!!!

--End

THE EAGLE SOARS
(A Song)

Flying so high above our land
Soaring proudly ever so free
Our great bald eagle, oh bird sublime,
Our hope, our strength, so endlessly
Come hither, come home, by water's edge
Now land upon some silken blade
From forest fair God gave to ye
To live within man's endless rage!!!

Oh,---

Our bird up high now in God's sky
Hath seen the hopes and joys of man
For as we sing our eagle's song
She guards us out and from within
Our great proud bird doth test our times
And keeps us safe from divorcive faith
She holds our keys to heavenly hearts
And grants us love in many a place!!!

Landing aloft high in God's hills
Far above our wants and cares
God's great bald eagle soars again
To bring us peace and strength to dare.
Its great "feathered coat" so full of shine
His proud bald head with gleaming pose
Shall all invoke God's sacred best
And prod us on to endless roles!!!

Oh,---

As eagles fly above our land
They come back hence to live and rest
Man in all his follies needs
To care for God's own birds and nests
For if this great bird lives today
She stands for strength and nature's pride
For all who see her at her best
Shall know she forth shall reside!!!

Oh,---

As I now end this eagle's song
And as I prepare to lay my pen
I shan't in all my eagle best
Forget her love she gave to men
For God and country doth resolve
That where our great bird lives today
Shall hold the keys to peace within
And give us love on judgment day!!!

Oh,---

Our bird up high now in God's sky
Hath seen the hopes and joys of men
For as we sing our eagle's song
She guards us out and from within
Our great proud bird doth test our times
And keeps us safe from divorcive faith
She holds our keys to heavenly hearts
And grants us love in many a place!!!

OUR COUNTRY MEANS A LOT
(A Song)

A great and mighty country
The land of brave and free
Nestled between two oceans
Just for you and me.
See tis what our God gave
In all His loving best
She tis land of glory
And sanctified the rest.

A heaven for the downtrodden
A refuse far and wide
The great land of Lincoln
Instilled with country's pride.
She's the best God has to offer
Our freedoms shall live on
And find their place in glory
This land we call our home!!!

From the mystic seashore
By the rocky hills
Stretching through the prairies
What a glorious will.
She t'was made for living
And giving all she's got
By the gates of heaven
She means an awful lot!!!

Time to end my love song
This warm and sunny eve
And not let me deceive you
For she tis love indeed.
For she tis real in glory
And she tis far from gone
Her colors will fly in heaven
As we sing our nation's song!!!

--End

FULL SPEED AHEAD
(America)
(A Song)

As we travel around this land
And visit each place in full delight,
As we wax older on this soil,
We shall not stop for day or night
For nothing short of poetry prose
Shall stop our country this land unbarred.
We build and grow with endless miles
And never let down our own guard!!!

Our country our nation from farms to towns
And cities of the great sublime
From hill and hollow and all around
We push our time and pace our line
We build with blocks and lay our bricks
Upon each other our souls in sway
And form a great and boundless deep
Of country with her love today!!!

From miles and miles of greenery turf
To mountains high with valleys low
From sea to sea and you to me
We push ahead with ceaseless tow.
And as our country, our land unbarred
Becomes the center of world affairs
We shan't in all our wondrous writ
Hold back our land God thus prepared!!!

This land, this country, this American soil
Holds forth the beauty of our hearts
And never pauses to pulse our time
But changes forth to form new starts
From sea to sea to time's own end
She'll be there when the hour comes
To give her glory in God's song
And be the all and all the one!!!

--End

WE PLEDGE
(A Song)

This day we hold within our hearts
A sacred, hallowed vow
A promise that shall never waver
A writ so cherished now.
This day we give back what we've got
And sanctify the rest
We pledge allegiance to our land
God gave to us His best!!!

This day we pledge within our hearts
God's grandest gift of all
A little handsome baby
To carry our race along.
We pledge to little children
To hold the highest esteem
To cherish our land with glory
And love our Christ, our King!!!

This day we pledge our honor
We have gotten from life
We lay it out completely
And pray to God by night.
We pledge within our hearts at best
To glorify His call
And give God all our talents
And word our rhyme with all!!!

This day we see the raindrops
Falling on life's way
But then we see God's angels
Lighting here to stay.
This day we pledge within our hearts
Our lives, our all, each man
This day we pledge allegiance
And take our Christ's own hand!!!

--End

OUR FLAG
(A Song)

Sewn by hand with many a stitch
Carefully given the stars and stripes
Our flag, our banner, Old Glory be
T'was raised aloft a pole with height.
Her cloth now flowed with wind and breeze
Lord, what a beautiful, awesome sight
Our flag hath adorned our American scene.

Oh,--

Our flag hath seen the best of days
Flying so high, the brave and free
Wrapping herself just like a lass
Keeping our hearts so innocently.
We exalt her in the best of times
We praise her in the battles won
And always love her in her best
For she tis all, and all the one!!!

Flying so high above our ships
Our flag hath seen our trying days;
She flew so high in battles thick
And saw us through some turbulent rage.
As poets draw their memoirs mix
She guards them through their tearful muck.
She serves us righteous in our days
And brings pure joy and desiring luck!!!

Oh,--

She looks so beautiful before the fall
With school yards open and children free;
She flies right by there on her pole
So bright and pretty as all can see.
For down at the courtyard square on one
She flies right there just by the door
And greets each patron with a sight
Of love and peace forevermore!!!

Oh,--

This song shall end before my time
And draw my heartstrings around my soul.
And choke the very verse from me
Of peace and joy and endless scroll.
For as I write about my flag
Her honor hath the thought in me
To rhyme her beauty, her vibrant verse
And love her tho I cannot see.

Oh,--

Our flag hath seen the best of days
Flying so high, the brave and free
Wrapping herself just like a lass
Keeping our hearts so innocently.
We exalt her in the best of times
We praise her in the battles won
And always love her in her best
For she tis all, and all the one!!!

--End

231

FLAG DAY
(A Song)

She hung there a'waving, moving ever free
I was just there watching, trembling in my knees.
Dad, with hand on heart, a teardrop from his eye
Mom, her hair a'flowing as our flag flew in the sky.

My brother's hand saluted our flag in all its great
My sister stood reciting our anthem from her slate.
The sky was sapphire blue and glory was the theme
Of Flag Day in Mississippi with the town folk on the scene!

The sun was climbing higher o'r our hometown place at large
Some little sweet old lady said, "Do you like my white corsage?"
I said, "Ma'am, I sure do. You look like God's own queen."
As the flag t'was just a'flowing, I licked some sweet ice cream!

The parade had all now ended; everyone was gone
And that very afternoon I sang our anthem's song.
Just a barefoot boy with flowers by the way
I stood there a'thinking, "What a glory time today!"

As evening shadows drew close, we sang our heartful song,
Strength from the Holy Bible we prayed for those who wronged.
And as Flag Day drew close, we said, "Our God tis grand!"
For giving us this Flag Day we all held each other's hand!

As writers pen their heartthrobs my flag tis flying high
O'r our own Mississippi with brilliance in God's sky.
And there I'll be a'watching with joy into my heart
For I love our own Old Glory by light of day or dark!!!

--End

232

VETERANS' DAY
(A Song)

Some say that freedom comes with the stroke of some new pen
Others say that liberty tis earned with works of men.
Still there are those who say that sacrifice and toil
Mixed with blood together are the rock of freedom's spoils!

There tis some young freshman in an Ivy college nigh
Searching through some papers saying, "Freedom's running high."
But let me tell you, Laddie, that there shan't a writ of man
That can hold our freedom if you "stick your head in sand!"

Freedom is earned with blood spilt upon some soil
Of a foreign nation that would like to see us boil.
For liberty's rock shan't start with some new pen
It is fought and earned by the blood of veteran men!

As I end my song, I'll look in God's own sky
At the eagle flying, watching us now go by.
And as I stand right there, I'll know in my own heart
That freedom came from love of veteran men embarked!!!

--End

FOREVER

Peering deep through depth and time
And through a mist of stars and seas
I perceive God's wondrous all
For, hence, His love hath come to me!

His greatness evoked the mighty currents
Of forever, endless space that ran
And sanctified time's enduring bless
And gave this fool his words at hand!

His great, his all, his endless night
Hath drawn man's hearts and minds to see
The forever, eternal, endless rhymes
Of poet fools like mine to be!

The awesome looks through scope and glass
Hath made God's stars a sight for me
I tremble before a heavenly host
Of Angels in their cosmic sea!

For God hath drawn His conclusive marks
Upon our deeds through thick and thin
And sent His son, His chosen best,
To sanctify the souls of men!

The eternal night that stands so wide
That covers the skies upon a sea
Of time's own endless, forever birth
Hath caused this fool his rhymes to be!

God's eternal fire that lights His skies
And Christ who comes to guide our way
This love, unbound, hath placed our hearts
Into His fold and His to stay!

For time and depth perceived by man
Shan't hold a grain of running sand
Into the forever, eternal night
T'was love, unbound, Christ took our hand!

THIS COUNTRY

This country, this country, amid the world so free
She's an angel for the masses
She's a heaven to the seas
She's a city in its glory
She's a drifter moving on
Unto this land of glory
How proudly we sing her song.

Oh,--

This country, this country, amid the stars and stripes
From the hills of California to the cornfields wide and bright
To the trolleys in New Orleans to the steeples of old San Fran
She's all and all there is, son,
She's freedom's time at hand!!!

This country, this country, by the water's edge
Closely to the heartthrobs
Of young men and their wed
By some country churches
On some campus free
This country, this country growing
Tis all and all to see!!!

--Oh,

This country, this country, heaven by the stars
Where the land is full of pleasure
Where the roads are full of cars
Where the postman puts his mail drops
Where the farmer builds his barn
This country, this land of plenty
Will protect all from the harm!!!

--Oh,

This country, this country, oh, her days are free
She's so strong and giving freely
She's the prayer upon our knees
She's the glory that God gave her
She's the "crier" in some hall
Shouting freedom's glory
This country shall never fall!!!

--Oh,

This country, this country, amid the trumpet's blare
Calling all who love her
Unto her loving care
Striving all to show her
That freedom costs so much
We should never waver
Unto some evil bunch!!!

--Oh,

This country, this country, amid the freedom's stars
Where God and Christ and Glory
Are her rock from far and far
Where the heavens shine their glory
And school kids board their bus
Where the writer's pen runs freely
Where the preacher asks a hush!!!

--Oh,

This country, this country, strong, proud and free
Amid God's band of angels
From sea to shining sea
Where we salute her glory
Where the outcast has a home
Until this land of freedom
How proudly we sing her song!!!

--Oh,

OH, WHAT A BEAUTIFUL DAY
(A Song)

As I gaze God's own awesome scene
With wind and sky and pounding sea
As I partake of nature's worth
Tis more than rhyme can come to me
I stare into the eternal sky
And, hence, wonder why life came to me
My God, my Savior, my forever birth
Tis all somewhere just waiting for me!
Oh, what a beautiful day, you say?
Tis what our Lord hath made today!!!

This time we spend in petty grieves
Tis like an ant upon some hill
So small, so tiny in meaningful worth
We scarce to see the rapturous fill.
But cast thy eyes upon God's plan
And cast thy net into God's sea
Now draw the fishes of everlasting man
Unto God's beautiful world to be!
Oh, what a beautiful day, some say
Tis what our Lord hath made this May!!!

The hour hand hath counted our hairs
Unto our hands with wrinkled skin
And God's wind, whips into our face
We hardly see the eternal end.
But stand and stare into God's "all"
And marvel what wonders come our way
The forever rhymes of fools like me
Shall fade away in judgment's day!!!
Oh, what a beautiful day today!
Christ hath come and paid our way!!!

As I end now my humble verse
Of land and sky and wind and sea
God's forever, ever, endless time
His stars and systems everlasting to be
I lay my tearful pen to rest
And garner up what time hath left
I rhyme with rhythm His chosen words
And sanctify His glories beset!!!
Oh, what a beautiful day this day
Lord, will ye come with Christ today???
And
Hold my hand and lead time's way!!!

--End

POET'S TIME

As days grow longer in their wealth
With little small minutes and hours past
Those precious monuments which God hath born
T'wer all for living and all for task
Those fleeting memories which catch our rhyme
Shan't all be lost in earthly jest
We'll jot them down on parchment fine
And word them proper with poet's best!

Each and every word t'wer spoken
Bars all the blame this writer's mind
Those haunting lyrics of masters old
Come rushing into poetic rhyme
And, lo, those words t'wer scribed with heart
Shall each and every one come bout
And give this soul his loving quest
To build and climb his sacred mount!

As days turn into years that pass
And time doth scare our very souls
We lift our eyes up from God's plan
And scan the earth in search of gold
But all t'wer naught and lost in time
Those years and years of "frivolous lays"
The only thing that shall forth last
Tis God and Christ and what we gave!

The sands of time embossed with pain
And rhymes and rhythms of those of old
Shall one day, hence, by no more
And leave our hearts to graves so cold
But as I speak a beam of light
Comes shining to my soul's array
Tis Christ who comes with outstretched hands
To pull me up and save my lays!

Those hours writing with earthly tasks
T'wer saved and placed into a book
Some with gold and parchment's leaf
And given God's approving look
The years of suffering had now ceased
My heart had flown into God's skies
Those years and years upon each rhyme
T'wer all now given God's master "bind!"

As I now end and lay my pen
Before my Maker's hallowed page
And garner up those promises kept
And gauge them each their rightful wage
I'll draw my last and fleeting rhyme
For Christ hath come and paid my way
And reached and took my trembling hand
And gave me life and saved my days!!!

--End

Introduction to "GOD IS"
William Furr

In writing this heartfelt poetic piece of work, I wondered and pondered long and hard, "Now what are the things that make God truly what He is?" As I began writing and putting on parchment the things that make God what He is, I soon realized that I could have continued on and on for 200 pages or 500 pages or 10,000 pages and never, ever really say all the things that make God what He is.

This poem is but my humble attempt to glorify and give honor to my greatest Master Jehovah God, as He is called, and to exalt and praise His Great Son, the Prince of Peace Jesus Christ, my Lord. I do hope that you, the reader of this humble lay, doth enjoy and become enlightened with the following verses of "God Is". May the Lord bless you and keep you and may one day all mankind find peace and happiness in the Great Master of all times, our Lord God, Creator of all things._____

GOD IS

--written for Christians everywhere

God is the starry sky
With all time spaced inbetween.
He is the glow of dawn
With light and the fresh-born spring.
From out eternity's bosom
Our God shall never die,
For He is all there is
And all what in doth lie!

God is the fruit on the vine
And He is the sunning rays
For God shall make the morrow
And all His works of age.
God shall hold our love thoughts
And never, ever, once cry
For He is the power of creation
And He is all our sighs!

God is the future tomorrow
And He is times gone past
For He is the looming presence
And He is the sun we bask.
Our God hath played his harpstrings
And born all that is
For He is now and forever
And He is all there is!

God is the tallest mountain
And He is the glacier's slope.
He is the sea and the seashore
And He is the hearts we broke.
God is the flesh we're living
And He is our very soul,
For He shall reign forever
And forever and ever we're told!

Our Lord hath been by sorrow
And He hath seen all strife.
He has been forever
And He has seen our blights.
God shall hold our measures
And He will count our souls
For He shall render judgement
Upon eternity's scrolls!

Our Lord hath drawn His pleasure
In creation by His will.
He hath seen the starlight
Above our fleeting frills.
He was here forever
And He is our just God.
A friend and Lord of ages
Throughout this earth we plod!

The rapture's dawn of infinity
The cosmos all in rhyme
And eternity's faintest starbeam
Are God and all His signs.
Forever and ever
From creation to the end
God is all there is
Which He hath right intend!

We human wax in wonder
As we gaze up to God's sky
That timeless, endless star-sea
Alive with all that lies.
For God is all tomorrow
And all our hearts attest
From out eternal treasures
And that we claim as best!

God is the beauty around us
And the dove high in its flight.
God is the great tomorrow
And the sky and the day and the night.
He is the glow of the sunset
And He is the new-found spring.
For God is the great creator
And He is our spiritual King!

God is the cloud and the rainbow
And He is the promise of love.
God is our greatest father
And He is our Lord above.
For God hath made all the lilies
And the roses upon this earth.
He is our mighty redeemer
Who gives us grace and worth!

God is the tallest mountain
And the valleys deep between.
He is our bountiful measure
Of all our earthly scene.
For God is the new beginning
Of all who seek His love.
God will never forsake you
For He is the Lord of love!

The hills and trees and wildlife
Are all God's wondrous hand
And all the deer in His thicket
He made to adorn this land.
For all the depths of the ocean
God placed into His sea
Life! For the every fisher
Who comes by Calvary!

God is the sea a'churning
From out the wind and lapse.
God is the eagle soaring
To highs we scarcely grasp.
God is the sun a'burning.
From time to eternity.
God is my ink a'flowing
So I might pen to thee!

God is the morn's awakening
From out the spring-filled night.
God is the cool brook flowing
Upon our hearts delight.
God is the face of tomorrow
And all there is at hand.
God is our grandest Master
With throngs of angel bands!

God is the eternal abyss
Across the starry night.
God is the moonbeam glowing
Upon our face tonight.
God is the quest forever
From time on time and end.
God is our hearts a'yearning
For peace and love towards men!

God is the eternal sunset
Which fires and lights our souls.
God is the great forever
And eternity's endless roll.
God is the grand beginning
Of all life and breath anew.
God is the rock of ages
For all who love Him true!

God is the small deer fawn
Huddled to its mother's breast.
God is the wind-lash blowing
Across earth's barren chest.
God is the snow in the meadow
So still and cold and clean.
God is the beautiful beginning
For all who claim Him King!

God is our eternal Master
Who guards and leads His fold.
He is the promised shepherd
Who went to Calvary's pole.
God is our eternal partner
Who loves us day by day.
He is our grand provider
Who gave His love to stay!

The cries of a creature in forest
And the owl and the wolf and the rest,
All are God's own beauty
For they are by God's wealth.
The trees and the pond and the vineyard
Were made by God's own decree.
He is our great creator
Who loves us endlessly!

Our God hath no beginning
And He shall never end.
He has been here always
And watches o'er His kin.
For God hath loved us humans
From out our tears and cries.
God shall draw His blessings
To all who claim His bride!

The rain that falls in droplets
And the stormy, turbulent sea
And gales of windblown fury
God made for man to see.
For all God's grandest pen strokes
Hath drawn this earth by hand
And granted each our rhythm
Upon time's endless sand!

The warm wind of God's springtime
And the cool blown breeze of fall
And all God's little lovenotes
Hath been blessed with all.
For God shall give His blessings
To each His life that bask
Upon eternity's landscape
From out God's blessed past!

God's lights from out His firmament
And into creation's dawn
And systems of starry space
Show us we're not alone.
And the flicker of time eternal
The lure of God's own plan
Holds each our door wide open
For all who grasp God's hand!

The spiral of a galaxy whirling
Into undaunting space
The power of all there is
Shows God is in His place.
The fall and then forever
And forever our Lord shall be
Eternal to His creation
And eternally shall He be!

God is our every tomorrow
Attuned to righteousness.
God is the kingdom of greatness
All born into Himself.
He is the rock of strength
For all who cast our sin.
God is the God of all
Who walk and talk with Him!

God is the glories of heaven
With all its beautiful berth.
God is the pulse of our hearts
From out their charitable worth.
God is the divine deliverer
Who pulls us towards His wealth.
God is our everlasting
Through sickness and in health.

As men into the night
Try in their follies' best
To explain away creation
And the encompassing rest
Our hearts of all we Christians
Hold fast to God's own truths
His saving grace and glory
Are there to see us through!

The moon hath cast a shadow
Upon some humble knave
And drawn him up to glory
Where God and angels stayed.
For Jesus hath but beckoned
All who trust in God
He shall never leave us
Of us who bore His rod!

The night grows cold and lonely
As poets fire their flame
To praise our great creator
And call upon His name.
For we in all our charity
Shall one day go to see
Jesus! God! In glory
Who loves us endlessly!

As little children playing
Adorn their innocent hearts
We, their own instructors,
Hath shown them by the start
God! And all His blessings
For those who walk in love
For little Tim and Alice
Shall raise their eyes above!

While soldiers fight with malice
And shepherds herd their sheep,
Man in all his diversity
Shall have a date to keep.
For once upon a heartbeat
Our Lord shall come to reign
And free and set His children
From their guilt and pain!

God is the fairest lovebeam
That rakes across His sky.
God is the newborn baby
With all its innocent cry.
God is eternal forever
With each of us in place.
God is the everlasting
Lord! Of wondrous grace!

God is the friend who surrounds us
And faithful Lord of old.
God is the divine physician
Who gives us health of soul.
God is the eternal matchmaker
Who pairs us with His love.
He is the one who brought us
Here! From out His love!

God is the celestial beauty
With each new sign of life.
God is the spiritual body
For all those lost in strife.
God is the great provider
For those who seek His love.
He is our Lord eternal
Who resides in heaven above!

God is the saving love grace
He is the Master of all.
God is the wealth upon us
He is our friend and call.
For God is the boundless seashore
That ferries across the night.
He is our ship of safety
And God is our spiritual light!

The earth holds each our heart strings
And raises all its men
Upon a sea of doubting
With all its fears and sin.
But God hath shown us humans
Life! So free at last
All for those who love Him
From out our works at task!

We humans strive to levy
Grief upon our souls.
But God, great God Almighty,
Hath seen our cares and goals.
God shall never leave us
Throughout our earthly home
For God hath rightly given
Love! For all that long!

The night burns on and restful
And all hath gone to bed.
Our clock is still on running
With tears our hearts hath bled.
For Christ shall come to raise us
Upon our final stance.
He shall pull our beings
From out the passing trance!

As days turn into years
And as our flesh grows old,
Men in all their hearts throbs
Hath turned their minds to soul.
For we God's creation
Doth know He loves us best.
We cling to biblical glories
And hope for all God's best!

God is our judge before us
He is our gauge of souls.
God is the greatest heaven
For all who strayed their fold.
God is the compassionate listener
For He shall calm the sea.
God shall always love us
From out His glories free!

God is the divine deliverance
In which He gives us worth.
God is the spirit that binds us
And saves us from this earth.
God is the hush of the night fall
In which His land has rest.
He is the morning's glory
In all his righteousness!

God is the farthest starbeam
Our eyes can surely see.
God is the ocean of stardust
Bequeathed eternally.
God is the mighty heavens
Of which this universe tis.
He is the grand creation
And all and all there is!

God is the craving for brotherhood
In which we humans seek out.
He is the feeling of compassion
Through earth and all about.
God is the God of our fathers
Which saved their souls unto
Time! And the eternal ravages
Which all must pass into!

William Furr

God is time's mighty sea surge;
He is the powerful wave.
God is the turbulent torrents
Of rain and sea at rage
God is the calm of euphoria
Unto our souls and rest.
God is the bestower of blessings
He is our everness!

God is the tallest pinnacle
Which juts up to the sky.
He is the deepest chasm
Where no man hath been by.
He is the rock of tomorrow
God is the love in our heart.
God hath no beginning
And He shall never part!

God is the grandest church
Which calls and praises His name.
God is the smallest chapel
In which our love proclaims.
God is the sky before us
By whence our prayers hath range
He is our personal savior
For all who bless His name!

God is the beautiful dandelion
Abloom upon earth's chest.
God is the fields of clover
Across earth's bountiful crest.
God is the mighty pine tree
And He is the singing brook.
God is the Lord of all
And He is our bible book!

Man shall never henceforth
Describe the space of time.
From out the dawns beginning
Our Lord hath placed His kind.
And forever shall God render
Grace throughout His place
That eternal, endless starsea
By whence we find our faith!

Our God is grand and saving
For God tis all our worth.
He shall make the pleasures
Of serving on this earth.
For time and then forgotten
Are each and all our flesh
The only things that last
Are God's and Christ's own best!

Our Lord through all the ages
Hath beckoned His great Son
To draw and give deliverance
And praise those souls who won.
For everyone that claimth
Jesus by their way
Shall bring God's starry wonders
To all who right obey!

God is strong and willing
He is all our might.
God is honey flowing
Into our hearts this night.
He shall reign forever
And God shall pave the way
Up to that grandest staircase
That leads to brighter days!

Upon some moonlite earth night
Our God hath brought His Son
Unto us humble humans
And given joy each one.
For Christ doth have the answers
For all who go astray
For Jesus is all and every
Love! Through gracious lay!

The little birds in bushes
And melons on earth vines
All are but reminders
Of signs throughout our time.
For God is the prophecy
And He is all our ways
Loving all His children
And pardoning those who stray!

By way of running earth tears
Our paths hath seen the way
Unto God's glorious heaven
With right and truth to stay.
For God is all our planning
For each of us called man.
He is now forever
And holds His flock in hand!

The time is right upon us
And Gabriel starts to blow
Time's triumph of the ages
And pull us from our woe.
For God is of the lasting
Life! For all who claim
Jesus! For the asking
And heaven in its reign!

As lovenotes from the Christ child
Our hearts are here to say
Glory! Unto His highest
And peace for all this day.
For God is grander power
He is all our worth.
Each we tottling humans
From out time's boundless turf!

God is the soul of conscious
Deep within our heart.
God is the pull of the spirit
By which all saving starts.
God is of some flower
A'bloom into His spring.
God is of the beauty
We each hath felt and seen!

God is the power of divinity
Which no man hath forsook,
God is by the rainbow
To wh ich we gaze and look.
God is of some pilgrimage
Into a distant land.
God is in His heavens
To which shall come His clan!

God is boundless space time
In which He holds us all.
God is in His heavens
With endless love to awe.
God is everlasting
Upon time's present reign.
God is there just waiting
For all who call His name!

God is of the sunrise
Glowing in its best.
God is of the brilliance
Of work and righteousness.
God is of some fairer
World in lovely lay.
God is for the asking
And all for us today!

God is of the sacredness
Unto which all things t'wer born.
God is real and loving
In our hearts so warm.
God is all description
Of everything at best.
God is all His starlight
From out eternity's quest!

Those years that wax upon us
Hold all our works proclaimed
And as we seek God's blessings
We each hath called His name.
For all and every love chore
And each small meager task
We toil for out our Father
And seek His will that lasts!

The days hold to their sorrows
Upon this rock of pain,
And God hath granted pardons
For all who love His name.
For God is of the morrow
And He hath given life
To each of His blessings
And all us in His light!

The sky is wide and open
And endless by the eye.
Eternity draws its entry
By whence we lived and died.
For the eternal tomorrow
Hath all our souls invest
Unto God's forever star space
From out our works and best!

God is the awesome beauty
We see before our eyes.
God is the harvest of souls
From out His son that died.
God is the cloud up high
He is the air we breathe.
God is everywhere
He is the one we cleave!

God is the majestic hills
Spaced with highest rims.
God is the longest river
Where no man dared to swim.
God is the grapes of vineyards
He is the fruit of the vine.
God is the hearts of many
For He is our Lord divine!

God is the seasons upon us
He is the mist of rain.
God is the warming sun rays
He is our Savior proclaimed.
God is the peace in the valley
He is the friend of all.
God is the reason for living
He is the earth's wondrous all!

God is the chill of winter
He is the snow and ice.
God is the whitest picture
Of serenity upon His flight.
God is the warming of springtime
He is the leaves on the vine.
God is the fields of beauty
From out His worth entwined!

God is the scenic mountain
Where only brace can climb.
God is the lovely hill range
Where pioneers brought their kind.
God is the forever beauty
Adorned upon this earth.
He is the master builder
Who brought us life at birth!

God is not allusive
He is not in vain.
God hath all the power
By which He works and reigns.
God shall guide His children
Upon from this world in time.
He shall never leave us
Nor ever change His rhyme!

God is wonders waiting
In which to bring this land.
God 'tis all the power
Of time, infinity, and man.
God is always near us
And He is by our side
Of all us striving Christians
Who claim His cross and bride!

The infinite quest of the sunrise
The soaring fowls up high
The dew on the distant roses
Hath all God's love inside.
The eternal, forever glories
That all must pass unto
Shall be the love for Christians
Who placed their souls anew!

Moving as some endless tide
Upon earth's bountiful crest,
Our God is a kindful Lord
Who knows what's good and best.
All allusive ones of human fold
Shall never get to see
God's wonderful, timeless, matchless peace
That comes from Calvary!

Those little things we deem as best
Are good and right for earth.
But fairer 'tis God's beautiful sky
Far from our cares and worth.
And greater, too, are things that last
Those things that set us free—
Love, acceptable, deepest faith
Forever! Shall they be!

God is all so wonderful
Throughout this rock of tears
And high above the floods of earth
We feel God through our years.
For God is all and He is just
And pardons all who stray
Into time's moving, endless surf
By forgiveness through His lay!

God shall rise above this scene
When all is said and done
And evil shall forth fall away
And victory shall be won.
And Jesus Lord so pure and right
Shall set our shackles free
And draw us up to new-found wealth
Forever! Endlessly!

God is as the provider
Giving all to earth
And little we of waning faiths
Hath ruined His nature's worth.
We cut the foliage and trample lives
And deed our wills be done.
Little do we stop to see
The harm that we hath done!

God our grander poetry is
Far from the earthly best.
For God hath rhymed the heavens
With genuine sacredness.
God draws upon His gift of words
And gives us thought in mind
And states His aims and eternal fame
And turns us loose to mind!

God is the friend we're seeking
And He shall be to the end
A fairest, loyal companion
A God to tell of our sins.
For God 'tis great and pardons
All who call His name.
God will in time deliver
Life! Eternal! And reign!

God is forever rhythm
In which He casts His love.
God is all our heart songs
From out His sky above.
God is of our beings
He made and born and saved.
God is all our lovebeams
In which our lives are gauged!

As God doth rhyme the heavens
With seas of starry sky,
Man in all his pondering
Hath seen God's wonders nigh.
And in God's endless time space
Are you and I and He
And all creation's room
From out eternity!

The wide berth of the oceans
And waves upon the shores
And starfish and the wealth
Are God's own gifts galore.
And days of timeful pleasure
Of songs from out this land
Hath sown us very humans
That God is love at hand!

We in our weakness cravings
Doth try our very hearts
And doubt and grope our way
Into some adventurous part.
For little do we wonder
What is our race at hand
'Tis God! The very being
That brought us to this land!

Those scars upon our foreheads
Hath shown our hard-pressed works
And all our aging memories
Hath drawn us by our worths.
For great God Almighty,
Shall one day bring to be
Glory! From out our winning
Each lost soul to see.

The poet comes to earth
Not by an act of chance
For God hath rightly chosen
Those to which enhance
His timeless, endless creation
In which He toiled and gave
To each we wayward humans
From out His saving way!

The order of all things
T'was born into God's plan
The acorn to the tree
And the dove above the land.
For life though brief it is
Hath shown God on this earth
Beauty from out time's bosom
And joy from out God's worth!

Into some abominable flight
The devil tests our souls
And tries to draw our beings
Away from Godly roles.
But we in all our frailty
Shall grasp the hand of Christ
And turn the devil loose
And set out hearts to light!

God is our Lord through ages
He is our saving King.
God is the greatest shepherd
He is our song to sing.
God is our ship of safety
He is our floating ark
High above earth's waters
From out we hath embarked!

God is the encompassing night
In all its moon-bathed glow.
God is the flowing fountain
From out this earth below.
God is the lasting wealth
Adorned upon this land.
God is the eternal King
Who loves us in His plan!

God is the time upon us
For He is the present and past.
God is the great tomorrow
For He is those things that last.
God is forever and ever
And He is creation's bliss.
God is our coming savior
In all His hallowedness!

God is the miles upon us
He is the road to our souls.
God is the pull of our heart strings
For He is the wonders of old.
God is the greeting tomorrow
He is our beacon of light.
God is our every beginning
For He is our hearts' delight!

We each in human follies
Hath drawn upon time's sand
All mementoes of heartbreak
And all our sorrows of man.
But God hath seen every teardrop
We humans hath shed in vain
For He will forthrightly deliver
Our souls from out our pain!

The hour is fast upon us
When breath and flesh shall pass
And time's ultimatum dictates
To each of us our last.
For every drop that falleth
Of dew upon this earth
There is God Almighty
Waiting with our berth!

The pressing invitations
To which our Lord doth give
Shall be time's final judgment
That moves us through the years.
For each and every challenge
We humans take in deed
Shall hold those keys to heaven
To which we shall receive!

As enormous as the sun
And as gentle as a doe
From out this infinite time frame
And forever and ever ago,
God has been here always
And He shall always be
Lord Of all creation!
By which we come to see.

The dawn hath moved tomorrow
Closer than we think
And time's own fleeting lurings
Shall pull us to our feet.
For now and then forever
Forever and ever shall be
Eternity! Without Savior
Jesus! Lord of me.

As acts of disobedience
Manifest themselves on earth
And perpetrate their presence
Upon man's honorable worth,
Some poem shall evoke
That for which God stands
Staunch, righteous and inviting
For all who take Christ's hand!

We sift through miles of archives
In search of that what is
And find God's beautiful springtime
As life is all that tis.
And turn within our beings
And discover all God's plan
His love filled inhabitated creation
From out eternity's sand!

Earth's scholars in their muttering
Hath scorned God's saving wage
That for what Christ stands for
And that for which He gave.
And in their thinked learning
They never once do see
around God's star sky
And eternal creativity!

Man holds to earthly rhythms
To which he understands.
He beams he holds the measures
To explain his plight at hand.
But, nay, shan't he be given
The power to rhyme the sea,
Only God Almighty
Knows our destiny!

God is all the history
By whence we come of age.
He 'tis as our Father
With love and generous ways.
For everything He granted
Shall one day cease to be
Except His saving Christ child
Who paid the eternal fee!

The tears of many poets
Hath flowed their rhythmic ways
Before eternity's creations
And gone to gayer ways.
And striving with conviction
Shall all our rhythms be
Jesus! God! Almighty!
From out His starry sea!

As tomorrow hath forsaken
Objects on this earth,
There 'tis grander glory
For each who claim God's worth.
And forever shall we reign
And forever shall we be
With our Christ in glory
From out eternity!

God 'tis as the heavens
Above all eyes and hearts.
God knows all the goodness
And He knows all our parts.
For God sees all His children
And He sees all who vain.
For all 'tis by some scripture
Man! In worldly games.

God is here forever
Through war and muck He reigns.
For God hath born our lives and all
And given miles of range.
For when the eternal writ is closed
And all has forever ceased,
There shall rightly be in store
Love! And eternal feast!

God is as the running brook
He is the cleansing tide
That boundless, flowing, ceaseless love
In which we draw to side.
And rhythms from out His invested lore
Shall all we earthlings see
The invitation in waiting arms
To save our souls for free!

Our God is as some sonnet
Flowing from out time's mirk
Through centuries past and present
God has rhymed His work.
For each and every beauty
God hath sent to man
All show God's ever goodness
For all who accept His plan!

The stormy rage upon time's shores
And waves that grip our souls
And fire throughout God's forever space
Are all God's wondrous roles.
And pulse and flesh and life abound
Are all God's glories great.
Even the tiny birds that sing
Were all made by His grace!

Those bells which toil for souls gone past
And miles of endless tears
And all the sorrows on this earth
Are not the Christian's fears.
For life and breath and joy of all
Is creation as God planned
All wait the child who walks with Him
Jesus! For every man!

The fool that pens there is no God
Shall never make the page
Of that grand book in which 'tis writ
The acts of Christians' wage.
For deed and prophecy and striving ways
All hold those golden keys
For all mankind in prolific rhymes
Forever! Endlessly!

From out this life of surging ways
And into time's infinite dawn
Through light years past and eternal days
We sing God's lovely songs.
For those who hold to righteous lay
And all who meekly see
God's lasting, never endless love
Shall find eternal glee!

God is all the vivacious
Light from out the sun.
He is the glory a'looming
To christen His hallowed Son.
God is the thunder a'rolling
And He is the driving rain.
God is the water of this life
For all who call His name!

God is the long-sought fountain
He is the youth for old.
God is the mighty Master
For He is the strength for souls.
God is the lamb a'sleeping
And He is the bread of life.
For God is the voice of His heavens
And He is the starry sky night!

God is the way to heavens
He is the calm in the storm.
He is the snow-capped mountains
And God is our creator adorned.
God is the rose in the valley
And He is the giver of souls
God is the granter of blessings
He is our provider from old!

God is the longing within us
He is the pull of our hearts.
God is the wealth of our blessings
And He is the soul who embarks.
For God 'tis the master craftsman
He has built mountains so bold.
And God is the breeze in the springtime
And He is the snow in the cold!

Our Lord hath ruled His heavens
With power no being can be.
Our God hath placed His starlight
To shine for all to see.
Our God hath born the ages
Of creation to this day.
God even made the sunshine
To warm us every day!

Our Lord hath been inventive
To make this ball called earth.
God even shaped the oceans
And gave them life and worth.
God made the sun-baked beaches
And gave them all so free
To each and every human
To enjoy endlessly!

God is all so merciful
In which He loves each man.
He placed us on this earth
And brought us life and land.
God molded and He shaped thus
Our nation full of pride.
He even gave us freedom
With liberty inside!

As days turn into months
And months turn into years,
Our God hath given His blessings
To all He loves sincere.
For God is all so wonderful
He is the greatest one
Who gave His Christ at Calvary
And paid the price and won!

God is the starry space sky
He is the abyss deep.
God is the Lord of creation
And He is our cherished belief.
God is the glow of the morning
He is the Master of our souls.
For God is the keeper of truths
He is our Lord to behold!

God is the fresh spring morning
He is the Lord of our hearts.
God is the maker of love songs
And He is the light through the dark.
God is the valley of sincerity
He is the comforter of life.
For God is the prophecy of ages
And He is the giver of sight!

God is the song of the robin
He is the anthem in rhyme.
For God is the hymn of our singing
He is our creator divine.
God is the path to eternity
He is the beholder of all.
For God is the worker of wonders
He is our strength when we fall!

God is our feast when we're happy
He is our hearts when we cry.
God is our drink of pure water
He is our spiritual guide.
For God is the giver of mercy
And He is the judge of all men.
God shall grade us by measures
And place us where our hearts hath been!

God is the beginning of mercy
To which our souls hath need.
God is the future tomorrow
In all its encompassing deeds.
God is the lily in silence
With its beauty all in bloom.
God is this wondrous earth
In which we people roam!

God is the rearing of children
To which we humans strive.
God is the little small chapel
Which holds our Lord inside.
God is the giver of food
To an earth and all its needs.
God is the small hungry child
To which we love and feed!

As time draws each our bodies
Into that grandest stand
Before our great creator
Beside His angels at hand,
We search and strive for victory
Before our breath hath ceased.
We all must see our Master
In which we all hath need!

As years press on in rhythms
And as our bodies age,
The grave shan't be our encore
Before eternity's stage.
Our souls hath been united
With love and all its wealth
For Jesus, Lord of Mercy,
Hath drawn us to himself!

God is the moving stardust
Upon the universe deep.
God is warmth and merciful
From out His loving feats.
God is of the Christ child
Who beckons all our hearts.
He is Lord of ages
And He is all our parts!

God is all for asking
Each man unto himself.
God is all deliverance
To which lost men hath wept.
God is there for each one
Who calls upon His Son.
God will never leave you
For victory shall be won!

Our Lord is truth and mercy
Upon this ravaged earth.
Our God is all our heart strings
To which we right exert.
For God is each and every
Love deed that we hath done.
He will wipe our teardrops
And place us by His son!

Our hours hath moved so quickly
Throughout our lives at best.
For Jesus Christ of Nazareth
Hath placed us in His quest.
And as the cock crows thrice
Each soul shall forth be stirred
And Gabriel shall come rightly
For Christians! With God's word!

The infinite glow of sunrise
The clouds all full in sky
And God, great God Almighty,
Hath born His creation nigh.
And each and every beauty
In earth and above time's sea
Hath all their grand beginnings
In God! Eternally!

The heavenly lights in the firmament
Glow throughout our nights
And God, great Lord of creation,
'Tis where our souls hath flight.
For one day upon God's reigning
All shall forth be placed
And find their newer quarters
Upon God's endless grace!

The breath of new-found beginnings
And the factual works of God
Hath all thus been recorded
By whence He bore the rod.
And we His grandest children
Who hold His truths shall rest
Upon the endless blue sky
With Jesus and His best!

The dawn from out the firmament
And the starry sky in space
And forever and forever
God gave His heart with grace.
For all we striving Christians
Shall one day get to see
Our greatest, grandest Master
Who loves us endlessly!

God is light beyond
Time's perpetual, awesome sky.
God is our breath in us
So that we live, not die.
God 'tis all our seed
Born out from creation's fold.
He is of the sanctity
And perfect in His role!

God is the fairer love beam
From out our hearts this day.
God is the joy of laughter
For each little child who plays.
God in the world around us
And He is of sacred soil.
God hath blessed this earth
In which we work and toil!

God is the flaming firmament
From out the dawn of time.
God is the work of love
He is the beautiful rhyme.
God is aware of our feelings
He is our Lord who knows
Our every move and measure
Throughout our precious souls!

God is the seas of Noah
In which He moved His might.
God is the heart of David
Who smote the giant in fight.
God is the strength of believers
And He is the bugler's blare
Before the Walls of Jericho
To which hath crumbled there!

William Furr

God is the coat of colors
And He is the fiery bush.
God is the Holiest of Holies
He is the mountain that shook.
God is the Ark of the Covenant
From out which Abraham prayed.
God is the lamb so pure
And He is the heart that obeyed!

God is the glory of highest
He is the angels that sing.
He is the mountain of olives
And God is the dove on the wing.
God is the parter of waters
To which He saves all men.
He hath laid our pathways
For all who walk with Him!

God is the love we shareth
By which we come of sight.
God is the child in the bullrush
And He is the widow's mite.
God is the staff of our fathers.
He is the fountain of old.
God is the sky of Golgotha
He is our Christ in His role!

God is the years upon us
And He is our spiritual call.
God is the one beside us
Who cares and loves us all.
God is now and eternal
And before the eyes of man.
God is our Savior in blessings
From out His wonderful plan!

God is a God of mercy
Whose brilliance tis our light.
God is a Lord of loveness
Who guards us day and night.
God is a God so gracious
Who cares for one and all.
God will match our giving
And protect us when we fall!

Great God, Jehovah Almighty,
Hath given this universe quest
To share His cherished blessings
And witness at our best.
For every soul that heedeth
God's plan for out this earth
Shall find their solace waiting
In heaven! With its worth!

God is the encompassing feeling
We hold within our hearts.
God sets us free with blessings
To follow His loving art,
And bids us in our rhythms
The best throughout our days
And sends His son from Calvary
To save us in His ways!

God hath built His bridges
For each lost soul to pass
And cross into His glories
With heaven within our grasp.
For it 'tis up to us--
We who hold the keys
To open up God's pearly doors
And bring our souls to He!

God hath paved the road
Which leads up to His home
With charity and forgiveness
For all who sing His songs.
And God hath parted wide
His stars from out His sea
To draw us close to Him
Eternally, endlessly!

God is great and powerful
And reigns above His lands.
God is grand and wonderful
And gave this earth to man.
For God 'tis all we're seeking
He hath pardoned me—
All who take His mercy
And love Christ endlessly!

As time moves to new quarters
We humans on this earth
Strive in daily work chores
To make our place and berth.
But little do we listen
To God's glorious plan
That for which he's given
To save the souls of man!

The comet travels silently
The stars burn on in time
And God, great God Almighty,
Hath given all in rhyme.
And we His earthly children
Hath seen what He hath done
And send our souls hereafter
To God's great, grandest Son!

God is all the goodness
From time's blessful works.
God is all the luring
To which our souls exert.
God hath moved His Christ child
To earth and lovingly shared
Salvation to each Christian
And peace to all our cares!

God is of some seashore
From out which man beholds
Washing time's beautiful beaches
With love for every soul.
God is but the high tide
Reaching within His grasp
Cleansing all His children
With warmth and love and laps!

God is every forest
Over earthly lands throughout.
God is every raindrop
Which cools and ends a drought.
God is all the wildlife
Which shows His presence nigh.
God is of the orchid
Abloom for every eye!

God is here among us
Before our souls to see.
God is our every being
He is a part of me.
God made into His image
Each soul that draws its breath.
He even made the star dust
Above our human self!

God is of the steeple
A'high into His air.
God is of some churchyard
And loves our souls in prayer.
God is grander glory
In which we all can board
And fly away to heaven
And find new paths to ford!

God is the glow of star lights
Born out from systems in time.
God is all the atoms
Which comprise our very rhymes.
God is all the total
Matter-- in allusive space.
God is in the proton
And all by His own grace!

God is all the refuge
In which we all can bide.
God 'tis tranquil places
To which we all shall strive.
God 'tis of the faint star
Beyond His forever sea.
God hath flung His light speed
From out eternity!

God is the grass in the meadow;
He is the trees that hang low.
He is the mountain before us;
God is the ice and the snow.
God is the road that windeth
Across the land through night
God is the sun that seteth;
He is the love of life

God is the day before us;
He is the sun that is high.
God is the earth wind blowing;
He is the lover's sigh.
God is the reason that two ones
Can pair throughout their lives.
He is the sanctity of marriage;
God is the love in His night.

God is the reason I'm writing
In my spiritual writ.
God is this calling within me
To praise Him by my script.
God is the power He's given me
This power, as I grow old
To love His Son called Jesus
And cherish my heavenly goal.

God is the leaves on His trees;
He is the flowers that bask.
God is the clear-running brook
And all the life that last.
God is the stars in His sky
This beautiful night, I'm told.
He is everlasting
Forever in His role.

God is the cool breeze blowing;
He is the hurricane's might.
God does things spontaneously;
He gives us love in the night.
God moves each my pen strokes
And tells me what to plod.
He even runs my ink well
Every time I start to nod.

God is the "Joy of the working"
As Kipling once hath said.
God is the Master Poet
Carousing with my head.
But shan't I loose my heartthrob
To tell me what to write.
I plod surely on and on
And pen just through the night.

God is the time of repentance;
He is the Holy Ghost.
God is the moving spirit;
He is the sinner's host.
God will save ye surely
Before the eyes of man
For all shall see a change
In tune with heavenly clan.

God is the Holy Altar
Where two doth give their heart.
He is the horn of decision;
God is the light in the dark.
God will surely save you
Before your time runs out
If you get to moving
And ask Him right and now.

God is the peaceful nighttime
All serene and quiet and still.
God is the crickets chirping;
He is all life fulfilled.
God is this fool a'toiling
Writing down his heart
Until Christ takes my hand
And leads me from the dark.

God is the coming rapture;
He is the trumpet's blare.
God is great and mighty;
He is our cross to bear.
God is the dimmest starlight
That shines throughout the sky.
He is the poem of glory
For you and He and I.

God is all our love;
He is our very hearts.
God is of our conscience
From Him we shant depart.
We love Jesus so much
That scarce I jot this line
Holding back my teardrops
In rhythmic rhyming rhyme.

God is the rose on Easter
Red and white and pink.
God is the pen I am writing
With hallowed sacred ink.
God is all I live for;
He is my all and joy.
What I pen for Jesus
Shall never once annoy.

God is the clear-running brook;
He is the mountain's stream.
He is the grandest river;
God has forever been seen.
From meadows to His flatlands
From mountains to His sky,
God has been here always
And forever by and by.

God is this conviction upon me
That moves my pen along
Time's awesome love notes
As I sing this hallowed song.
God is the reason I'm living;
Without Him I'd be lost
In a sea of mankind
Without a chance or thought.

God is the grapes in the vineyard;
He is the sycamore tree.
God is the "Mount of Olives;"
He is the Calvary.
God is the flowering dogwood;
He is the wheat in the field.
God is nature upon us;
We marvel at His great will.

God is the chapel's music;
He is the tolling of the bells.
God is the harp and the organ;
He is the "song of the dell."
God brought us His music
His lyrics I've been told
From organ to piano
And expound His heavenly goal.

God is the rain that hath fallen;
He is the clouds in His sky.
He is the lightning flashing
God is the tears in our eyes.
As we marvel at creation,
We humble within our task
That God hath created eternity
And all and all that last.

God is the evening upon us
With all its special time.
God is the power of glory;
He is this rhythmic rhyme.
God is the night that befalls us;
He is the cool of the eve.
Whatever we do for Jesus
Shall last throughout this read.

God is our friends among us
Those whom we hold close.
God is our pastor preaching
Expounding what God hath wrote.
God is the sermon to us;
His words of rhyme hath ran.
God is the poem before me
All written in His own hand.

God is the age we live in;
He is this nation at hand.
He will not forsake us
As these words of rhyme to man.
God is all the grandest;
He is all I am.
A foolish poet this night
Intuned with heaven's clan.

God is the "rock of ages";
He is the seven seas.
He has been here forever;
God is the one to believe.
God has miles of pen strokes
From poet fools like me.
What I pen in earnest
Shall haunt me eternally.

God is good and kind;
He has a very large heart.
What He does for mankind
Shall save us from our dark.
What God does in earnest
Shall make our days at large.
God is glad and happy
When we board on "Noah's Ark."

God is all our facts
Those deeds we learned in life.
He is kind and merciful;
God loves man now outright.
He is all our being
For He is our very soul.
I love God so humbly
That scarce I rhyme this role.

God is in our midst
For He is the nearest tree.
He is the bush and the flower
For all the world to see.
God is all our wants;
He is all our cares.
What we do for Him now
Shall carry our cross to bear.

God is the awesome nighttime
Some heavenly night of old
With stars and seas of planets
And comets' tails to behold.
God is the time between them;
He is the eternal wind.
God brought love to stardust
And all things including men.

God is the power of His word
Those stories that tell it all
To give us His Bible
For each of us and all.
For if we read His scriptures
We, in time, will see
Peter and the gates of heaven
And all time's glory.

God is the power of conviction
By which we Christians move.
God is the spirit a'plenty
By which we spread His news.
God is the force within us
That pays our every way
To the gates of heaven
So very, very far away.

God is the "pull" of this lyric
All decked in rhythmic rhyme.
God is the power of pen strokes
All worded in every new line.
God is the talent that befalls me
A gift, so I've been told
To rhyme His heavenly messages
This starry night so old.

God is this piece of paper
From out which holds my writ.
God is the flower growing;
God never stops or sits.
He is my Heavenly Father
And He knows all the best.
With rhyme I doth respond to
Through earth's eternal test.

God is the daytime hour;
He is the nighttime, too.
God is love unbounded;
He is peace in tune.
God gives each His sheep
Miles and miles to graze.
He gave me my paper
And forever made me saved.

God is the gift of the lyrics
As is the Master's news.
He is the All and Mighty;
God is the righteous views.
God is the Lord forever
And as Lord shall He be
The All, the Great, the Mighty
Throughout all eternity.

God is the poem of sanctity;
He is the lyrics on line.
God is the thought I'm conveying;
He is the poetic rhyme.
God is the reason for living
And living shall He be.
Our eternal forever ever after
In time's endless sea.

God is this task before me
To pen just out my heart.
The earth's own longest poem
To save men in their dark.
God gave me this challenge
To scribe this line as one
To bring ye to the Christian
And save ye one on one.

God is the hour before us;
He is the Biblical treat.
We give Him our offerings
With cheer and joy—repeat.
God passes His own blessings
To those who give their all.
He builds them a new cathedral
In heaven's God-filled halls.

God is the sky above us;
He is the fartherest space.
God gave us this earth home
And admonished us with His grace.
God gave us His Christ Child
To save us one by one.
If we only accept Him,
Our battles will be won.

God is the poet's love dream
That inspires our pen to move.
Telling man of Jesus
And all that does behoove.
God is sanctity for us
If we ask His way.
Unto this world of sinners
He'll love us each new day.

God is this age of progress
As mankind makes his way.
Before a host of follies
All entwined in disarray.
God gave us our earth jobs
But, nay, we do our own
Rejecting what He gives us
And go off on our own.

God is the young girl;
He is our family's pride.
God has a place in our hearts
Where He hence forth resides.
God is the grasp of the moment
For He shall call us home
Before a band of angels
On and on and on.

God is the moon and the heavens;
He is the sun and the stars;
God is the universe spiraling
Throughout all time at large.
God is the all and forever
And all stardust at hand.
He will guide my pen strokes
As the words of rhyme hath ran.

God is the snowflakes falling
He is the blizzard's breeze.
He is the chill of the morning;
God is the winter's siege.
God brings forth His Christians
To comfort and give us peace.
He hath brought forth His Christ Child
With arms outstretched to reach.

God is the little lovebirds
All huddled in their little nest.
God is the eggs a'laying
To hatch new lives at best.
God is the clock a'stroking
To pace me of my rhyme
Jotting down on paper
Forever for all time.

God is the sea of mankind
All spread around this earth.
God is the scented flower
Which gives a scented mirth.
God is the waters flowing
Through valley and river's dell.
God gives each new waters
To cleanse man of his hell.

God is the time of prophecy
From Biblical text so old
To bring forth His great rhymes
To remind man of His goal.
God holds each accountable
Of all our earthly ways.
What we do for others
Shall determine our eternal stay.

God is the heavenly rapture
Upon whose souls shall rise.
God is Gabriel's trumpet
Which sounds throughout the skies.
God is the Christ Child coming
To claim His heavenly flock.
God is this chosen lyric
To expound what heaven hath got.

God is the time upon us
With deeds, in part, to do.
God is the mission given
To right this world anew.
God is the challenge to us
To tell the truth of Christ.
God is all the forever
First and never the last.

William Furr

God is the morning's glory
With skies so blue and white.
God is the nighttime on us
As I continue to write.
God is my burning desire
To word this hallowed page.
God is the reason I've living
To expound what Christ doth say.

God is the mission upon me
To write this rhyme at length.
God is all my being
As I use each bottle of ink.
God gives me the stamina
To continue this sacred writ.
God has called my mission
And word Him with my lips.

God is the Master a'calling,
His voice so clear and sharp
To tell His children of Jesus
And all what He has got.
For Jesus holds those keys
To His own pearly gates
Unlocked but for the moment
As time doth slip away.

God is the cripple walking;
He is the blind that sees.
He is the leper's body
All pure and white and clean.
God is the time upon us
To gather our rhymes today
And make them count for Jesus
Miles and miles away.

God is the fartherest star glow
From out His universe fair.
God is the Great Forever
To rid us of our cares.
God shall not rebuke us
If we so trust His Son
Jesus Christ of Nazareth,
The Great Begotten One.

God is miles of pen lines
From out this poet's rage
Penning by the lamplight
Each sacred hallowed page.
God is my own talents
He put forth in my hand
To draw the things that matter
As words of rhyme hath ran.

God is the church forever;
He is the hope of man.
He hath given His children
Hope to join His clan.
He and Christ our Master
Shall one day see us through
Heaven for the asking
Just for me and you.

God is the writing poet
Penning out his lines
From John to Peter to Paul
Engrossed in rhythmic rhyme.
God is what you strive for
As evils muck the day.
The day and eternal forever
His love is here to stay.

God is the roses' fragrance
Which lures every scent.
God is the Grand Provider,
His Son He willingly sent.
God is the ink a'flowing
From out this chosen page.
God shall not forsake us
If we pay our earthly wage.

God is love a'bountiful
From out the poet's rhyme.
God is peace and compassion
Through eons wrought in time.
God is the one and forever;
He is the chosen King
To lead and guide and direct us
As "Hark, the Herald" sings.

God is the book on the shelf
Some Bible I've been told.
He is all the verses
Which held our very souls.
He gave us His Revelations
From Genesis to the end;
He has taught us truly
His Word shall never end.

God is the net in time's sea
Pulling in man's catch.
He is all our wishes;
He is our eyes that wept.
God is this very poem
Upon which we realize
That rhymes the heavens away
Before our very eyes.

God is the ravine canyon
So wide and long and deep.
God is all the moon beams
Which light our every sleep.
God is the tears a'flowing
Down some lost soul's cheek.
He shall prepare our quarters
And give us miles to seek.

God is all the animals
From out the jungles thick.
God is all the fowls
Protecting their little chicks.
God is this own poet's
Pen within my heart,
Wherever comes the lyrics
Shall be the rhyme to start.

God is the time of repentance
Upon which holds that key
To open the gates of heaven
And escape a burning sea.
God wants all His children
To be there by His side.
If we only claim Him,
In paradise we shall reside.

God is the highest sea wave;
He is the rolling tide.
God is the seacoast stretching
As poets pen their lines.
He shall exhalt the heavens
And cause His earth to cease
And draw those thoughts expounded
As Christ doth stand to preach.

God is the all and forever;
He is time's own span
Stretching from stars up high
Eluding our every man.
God is grand and powerful;
He is the galaxy's seat
With life and love a'bountiful
From out His greatest fleet.

God is the "Book of Life"
Embellished throughout His text.
God is "Hark the Herald"
Where two souls have forth met.
God is the voice within us
That says that all is not right.
He is our soul of conscience
And gives us love at night.

God is the seas a'foaming
With waves so tall and wide.
He is the seagull cries
Above our beach in stride.
God is the beautiful starfish;
He is the oyster shell.
God is all the sea life;
He is far from hell.

God is the "Drink of Life"
That quenches one in his thirst.
God is the book of souls
Of all of those who trust.
He is the beautiful rainforest
With trees of every type.
God is the one who mourns
Those lost souls of the night.

God is the moving force
Of power and mighty strength.
He is the grand pen writer
Who guides us in our "think."
God is the awesome heavens
With lights so far and dim.
He is the all and forever;
He'll be to the end.

God is the "Lord of Lords;"
He is the "King of Kings."
He is the one who gave
Us rhyme and rhythms to sing.
God will always be near
Until the judgments call
And Christians fly up to glory
And find their "Master's" stalls.

God is the blown breeze
Upon our backs of sweat.
God is the one who loved
Least we shall not forget.
He is the rapture, too,
And Gabriel's trumpets call
The All, the Great Forever,
In His great kingdom's hall.

God is the acorns falling
From out His forests' trees
God is the wildlife stalking
Before the winter's siege.
God is the waters churning
With caps as white as snow.
God is the grand finale
Amid the heaven's glow.

God is my pen a'writing
Jotting down His lines.
God is my paper glowing
Full of loving rhymes.
God is the Bible's cover
Which holds His sacred words.
God is the truth a'calling
To ask us if we've heard.

God is the brilliant sky
Amid the sunset's glow.
God is the bellowing clouds
Amid a blizzard's snow.
God reigns here forever
And forever shall He be
The All, the Great Redeemer
Which casts time's eternal sea.

God is the mighty continent
By which some earthquake moves.
God is our freedom's standing
For each of us to choose.
God is the grazing wildlife
From out some jungle's thick.
God is the night a'coming
As we blow the candle's wick.

God is the grandest sunset
Red and hues of orange.
God is the great instructor
Who lead us by the arm.
God guides us through
The times that lie ahead
God is the peaceful nighttime
As sleep doth lay our heads.

God is the white-washed seacoast
With life that adorns the beach.
God is the fishes of mankind
Which allude our every reach.
God brought mighty thunder
To a rainy sky.
God opens forth His arms
To receive us as we die.

God is the thick of battles
Fighting Satan's rage.
God is the judging redeemer
Who grades us by His gauge.
God was here forever
And forever shall He see
Our every trying moments
Who loves us endlessly.

God is eternal rapture
That takes place in His sky.
God is the judging everafter
While sinners therefore cry.
God is the awesome pen stroke
From poet fools like me.
God is the reign of glory
From out time's eternal sea.

God is the Ark of the Covenant
All laden with sheets of gold.
God is the Ten Commandments
That Moses carved so old.
God is the ark of Noah
All floating in perilous seas.
God is the blood of the land
For all, in Christ, to seek.

God is the Bible prophecies
All written in holy text.
God is the Temple of David
And the Gardens of Babylon next.
He is His ship on the water
Bound for His eternal sea.
He is the very essence
That fools, like me, pen free.

God is the "Hark the Herald;"
He is the wide Red Sea.
God is the Land of Canaan
He is the one we seek.
God is the lightning flickering
As fools as I pen on.
God is my every inspiration
As I rhyme His hallelujah songs.

God is the road to Damascus
Upon which Paul hath trod.
God is the sick man standing
Carrying his once-needed bed.
God is the Holy of Holies;
He is the Gift of Life.
For all who seek shall find Him
And confess their sins this night.

God is the aging poet
He is the fresh-born King.
He is the force that prods us
On with rhymes so keen.
God is the reason I'm living
To pen His words so bold.
He is the Lord of Lords;
He is the King of Souls.

God is the Land of David;
He is the nets in the seas.
He draws in His fish
Of souls that all hath need.
God is the Mount of Olives;
He is the sycamore tree.
He is the reason I'm living
To expound His prophecies to be.

God is the night growing longer
As lines keep coming my way.
He is the very reason
That I hath life today.
He is my thoughts a'coming
As lyrics move with might.
God is the reason I'm penning
This hallowed, sacred night.

God is the cloud in the heavens;
He is the lark on the wind.
He is with His angels
While earth doth wait its King.
He is the one who gives us
All, and then, some more.
He is the bread that sustains us
As we pen His Biblical lore.

God is this verse a'scribing
On this paper tonight.
God is this pen a'moving
With holy creative might.
God is the very reason
That I am here with Him.
Penning what He tells me
I'll do right to the end.

God is the mighty current
From out the ocean's roll.
God is this fool a'writing
This starry night of old.
God is the love within us
That shows we are kind.
God is this poem forming
In total rhythmic rhyme.

God is the late night hour
By which this poet writes.
God is my pen and paper
And the candle's dim weak light.
God is the voice within me
To expound what He doth say.
God is His love on paper
Forever and a day.

God is the storm out at sea
He is the calm of the lake.
Our God doth reign forever
Forever and a day.
Our Lord is great and mighty
And superior shall He be.
Our God, our hope, our refuge
Throughout time's eternity.

God is the stars in the skies
He is the glow of the moon.
He is the galaxy reeling
He is the night and the moon.
God never stops from doing
Forming His universe large.
He hath been here forever
Forever shall He lodge.

God is one voice within
That shows us what is right.
God is our spirituality
To comfort us in the night.
God is the Master Planner
To lay His earth in place.
God is the Grand Provider
That gives us each new day!

God is the "Rock of Ages"
He is the present and past.
God was here forever
And forever shall He last.
God grants each one our freedoms
He gives us of His time.
So foolish poets as I am
Can sing in rhythmic rhyme.

God is the time upon us;
He is the all and the great.
He has been here forever
And never locks His gate.
Time's own eternal firmament
T'was born from His great hand.
If we only trust Him
Forever we'll be in His clan.

God is the little small animals;
He is the love in their eyes.
He watches, each, His children
And grants us His great sky.
God has given the pen strokes
To me His humble rest
To rhyme His infinite heavens
And always be my best.

God gives each His poets
The rhyme to word His songs.
He gives us, His children,
The feeling that we belong.
God is the Grand Conductor;
He leads His singers at best
His voices and His lyrics
To sing and exalt His rest.

God draws my own love notes
From out time's eternal forces.
God guides my direction
To voice my rhyming score.
He is the Almighty;
He is my eternal glee.
All I have to receive Him
Is pay one small priced fee.

God is this writer's demeanor;
He is my mind and my soul.
God is my heart and my treasures;
He is the one to behold.
God give me the power
To convey what I do best.
If you want the same thing,
Just ask Him by request.

God is the words from your lips
If you praise His name.
He is the "Rock of Gibraltar;"
He is the name of time's frame.
God is all and forever;
He shall part time's seas.
He is the love in the beginning
For you and me to believe.

God is the cloud in earth's high sky;
He is the wind and the breeze.
God is the snowflake upon us;
He is all to believe.
God is the flower and meadow;
He is the golden rod.
God was here a long time
Before this poet's plod.

God is the Bible we open;
He is the scriptural love.
God was here before us
And He will be ever more.
God is the hearts and flowers;
He is the valentine day.
God brings two together
To guide and direct thou way.

God is the tree in Earth's forest;
He is the hawk on the limb.
He is the bark and the tree;
He is this sinner's pen.
God grants each, His children,
Miles and miles to roam.
He wants each and every one
To live in His big home.

God is the bridge over waters;
He is the stabilizing force.
He brought tides to sea coasts;
He is man's eternal source.
God is forever and forever
And forever shall He be.
The Grand, the Great, Almighty,
Throughout time's eternal sea.

God is the winter a'coming
As little lives stock their food.
God is the cool breeze blowing
As I doth pen His rules.
He gives us miles of freedoms
To see what we shall do
To earn our very salvation
The way He'd want us to.

God is this writer's mind
A'muck in worldly trance
Jotting down his sonnets
As though at first one's glance.
God is the core of the apple
All seeded with life to born.
God is the tall tree growing
In eternal beauty's form

God is the spirit that moves us
From rhymes to rhythmic stance.
God is the sonnets a'coming
As if though in some trance.
God is the reason we're living
To pen as we grow old.
God is the lyrics a'coming
So man shan't sell his soul.

God is the rainy nighttime
As thunder rolls along;
God is this fool a'writing
All nestled in his little home.
God is the poet's love dream
From out time's impermeable trance.
God is rhymes a'falling
Wherever there'll be a chance.

God is the age of Hercules
He is the house on the rock.
God shall not forsake us,
We Christians though time doth rot.
We leave our earthly bodies
To wax as they grow old.
And fly right up to heaven
To receive our eternal souls.

God is the cross on the hill
That stormy rainy eve.
God is the Master dying
So earth might get reprieved.
God is the shroud of the tunic
That covered our Christ our Lord.
We shall bear Him witness
That all this in accord.

God is the master plan
The script that I've been told
That planned us in the beginning
To pardon our very souls.
If we only accept Him,
We'll live forever today
Along the grandest stardust
Miles and miles away.

God is the hour long;
He is the second hand.
He converts the sinners
To place them in His clan.
He will not forsake you
In your deepest needs.
He is righteous justice
For every one to heed.

God is my soul a'burning
To pen what out I may.
God is my Christ, Redeemer,
As I write my poems today.
God is all the influence
To expound what He doth say.
The thoughts keep coming on paper
Though He is far away.

God is the star-struck heavens
From time to time's own end.
God is the fartherest galaxy
Born out from fire within.
God is the trail of the comet
That plods the heavens away.
God is all these lyrics
That rhyme and rhyme away.

God is the ocean brimming
With life from out the depths.
God is the tall sky beaming
As this poet tearfully wept.
God is the wildlife hearing
In forest and jungle scenes.
God is this writer learning
What life doth emphatically mean.

God is the love in our eyes
As we doth spy our mate.
God is the writer penning
This rhyme tonight so late.
God is the angel's call
Before we go to bed.
God bears His own witness
To tell us what we've said.

God is the winter's snowflakes
That adorn Earth's peaceful night.
God is the children a'beaming
As Christmas comes tonight.
God is the Christ Child laying
In hay all snuggled away.
God is this fool a'writing
To expound what Christ doth say.

God is the empty tomb
Upon which Jesus lay.
God is the Prince of Peace;
God is this poet's ways.
God reigns here forever
And forever may He say,
"What thou doest for others
Shall provide thy heavenly day."

God is this tearful poet
Full of words to write
To place down on white paper
What Christ doth say outright.
God guides my own pen strokes
To tell the world at best
"What thou doest for others
Shall be thy eternal rest."

God is the early morning
From out which poets rise
To rid this earth of stardust
And draw what he doth prize.
God gives each new morning
The words to govern our ways.
He shall lead us surely
To heavenly, righteous lays.

God is the storm a'brewing
Across some midwest key.
God is the lightning flashing;
He is the wind in our eyes.
God gives each, His awesome,
Lays to guide our way.
If we only mind Him,
Heaven shan't be far away.

God is the late night's candle
A'burning so I can write.
God is this poem forming
To bring love to the night.
God is the ink left drying
To word this hallowed page.
God is the moonbeam shining
Upon which hearts doth bathe.

God is like the wind
Which alludes our every reach.
God is like the seacoast
Along some dreamer's beach.
God is like the fruit
A'hanging from some vine
God is like my sonnet
A'tuned in rhyme after rhyme.

God is the highest hilltop
From which all cattle graze.
God is the flowered meadow
With lilies and petunias and sage.
God is beauty and serenity;
He is all there is.
He will be here forever
As I write this poetic quiz.

God is the markers a'stretching
Through fields of past-gone times.
God is this poet writing
With lyrics and rhythmic rhyme.
God is this poem a'burning
Without my soul at best.
God is the reader reading
This verse and all the rest.

God is the mighty stardust
Throughout all time that ran.
God is the awesome space time
He gave to each his man.
God shall never surrender
His stance for just and right.
He hath saved our starved souls
Until there comes the night.

God hath given this nation
His all, His best to test.
To see how each we use it
Shall be His finest best.
God shall hold our heartthrobs
Until we go to Him.
Jesus Christ, our Savior,
Will be here in our end.

God is the burning desire
Upon which all doth seek.
God is the heaven's love songs
Rhymed in a rhythmic beat.
God has given His own Son
To die for all our sins.
If we only accept Him,
We'll be there to the end.

William Furr

God is the new tomorrow
As sunshine rakes time's sky.
God is the breeze a'stirring
As tears invade our eyes.
God is all the emotion
Bottled within my pen.
He has been here forever
Forever before all men!

God is like the inkwell
Slowly being used
To put His love on paper
And read His timely news.
God is like my paper
All pure and white in part.
God is like the rainbows
Alluding our very hearts.

God is rain a'falling
From out summer's skies.
God is the moon a'shining
For He is the love in our eyes.
God is the great tomorrow
All encompassed and so grand.
His is all that matters
As the words of rhyme hath ran!

God is this nation a'moving
From out its past-gone times.
God is righting all wrongs
With love and respect in line.
God has given us this freedom
We each hold dear to start.
God is the coming cleansing
Of life and soul and heart.

God is the beauty around us
That surrounds this writer's pen.
God is this poem a'burning
From out all women and men.
God has given me those words
To pen to each His kind.
This poem tis the work of Lord God
And not this poet's lines.

God is the fartherest planet
From out the Milky Way.
God is the fiery sunset
Who warms life every day.
God shall never leave us
If we hold true to Him.
Jesus Christ, our Savior,
The Savior of all men.

God is the forever space time
From out all endless bliss.
God is the roaming comet
Earth hath narrowly missed.
As God hath made the stardust
He hath made each we
In His own likeness forever
to serve Him endlessly.

God is the awesome heavens
Upon which all life rest.
God is the forever and forever
With love He gives His best.
God hath moved the planets
Into their proper place.
God hath given us moonbeams
To light us with His grace.

God is the rolling wave
Pounding on some beach.
God is like the mistletoe
Just out human reach.
God is not elusive;
He is here to ask.
All you do is pray to Him
And open your heart at last.

God is the mighty fisherman
Pulling in His net.
Full of human souls so fast
The Devil loses his bet.
God gave us all His fishes
And sorts them one by one,
Turns them loose in new waters--
The freedom has been won!

God is like the falling rain
A speckle of stardust anew.
God is like the comet's trail
Across the heavens once flew.
God is grand and wonderful
He is all our hope.
All you do is love Him
And remember what I wrote.

God is the grandest melon
Growing on the vine.
God is like the garden
With stalk and fruit and vine.
God grows on you slowly
And He is, oh, so free.
A bargain for the hunter
Asking just one fee.

God is the grass a'growing
Throughout some meadows green.
God is the wildlife a'flourishing
From out time's endless scene.
God is the grand provider
Who gives and takes His best.
God will be here forever
This poet shall never rest.

God hath seen His stardust
Upon the Milky Way.
God hath fired the comet
To range throughout time's way.
God is the awesome space time
From out this poet scribes.
God hath humbled me truly
To claim Christ for my bride.

God is like the lyric
Expounded by some rhyme.
God is like the sonnet
In tune in rhythmic rhyme.
God has seen the wonders
Of His great creation fair.
God has given us each
No more than we can bear.

God is the ark a'floating
In floods of times gone past.
God is the animals a'clawing
To adorn His hills at last.
God replenishes starlight
Across the infinite sky.
He is all and forever,
And He shall never die.

God is the lightning striking
Some tree at edge of land.
God is the raindrops falling
As the words of rhyme hath ran.
God is the clock a'ticking
The minutes and hours away,
Only a second in glory
Throughout the Milky Way.

God is our precious liberties
All earned with sweat and blood.
God is our own heartland
Alive and undisturbed.
God is like the bridge span
Stretching from land to sea.
God is our own sunset
Impressive for all to see.

God is the Statue of Liberty
Holding up its torch,
Greeting all who see her
With freedom, love, and worth.
Those who came so far
To them we take their hand.
For God is like the Christian
Our witness for fellow man.

God is the awesome nighttime
Alive with specks of light.
God is like the sparrow
Asleep in its own right.
God is like Lord Jesus,
Our Messiah and Shining King,
Redeemer of all the World,
As "Hark the Herald" sings.

God is endless crosses
Across some "Flanders Fields."
God is all who seek Him
In war and battles grim.
God is high above
The eagles in His flight.
God will not desert us
Throughout our trauma's night.

God is snow a'melting
Running down Earth's crest.
God is the mighty river
So full it wants to crest.
God is the hill of timber
So green and tall and still.
God is like the lightning
That strikes Earth at its will.

God is the desert a'stretching
Beyond your wildest dreams,
Going on forever
With cactus and sandy scenes.
God is high in mountains
For He is at His best
Covered all with white snow
Upon some winter's crest.

God is the wildlife roaming
From plain and jungle mount.
God is the night a'crying
With life from out His "fount."
God gives life to seekers
Those who seek His love.
God will not forsake you
From out His stars above.

God is the burning desire
In poet fools like me
To pen His timely fashions
Upon some dreamer's sea.
God is like the vineyards
Full of grapes of life.
God is like the firefly
Glowing throughout his night.

God is the "fruit of the vine"
From out which all life feasts.
God is the milk and honey
For each of us to seek.
God has been here forever
Through time's well-worn path.
He will see us through
The Devil's evil wrath.

God is the flowers blooming
With blossoms and scented myrrh.
God is the rose a'growing
From out time's endless Earth.
God is the eagle soaring
Up high above earth's chest.
God is the moon a'shining
As earth doth go to rest.

God is the eternal forever
Upon which life t'was born.
God is the awesome heavens
For He is the night and the morn.
God has been here forever
And forever He shall be.
The all, the past, the present
And all our future's glee.

God is the rain a'falling
From out time's endless skies.
God is the running love brook
From which all lovers cry.
God is the strong emotions
Upon which rest our loves.
God has brought us our redemption
From out His endless love.

God is the lyrics a'rhyming
From out some poet's berth.
God is the spell of all things
That come and go with worth.
God hath seen the poorest
And riches of this Earth.
He shall make the Christian
To leave this temporal Earth.

God is the grandest flower
Which adorns some meadows fair.
God is the blooming rosebud
With beauty and scent to wear.
He shall range time's heavens
And provide what He hath made
To comfort all who seek Him
Throughout all eternity's rage.

God is the light a'shining
Across our frigid North Pole.
God is the One who gave us
His arms outstretched to hold.
God watches each of us
Throughout our fleeting lives.
He will not relinquish
His deeds, He does, tonight.

God stands strong for mercy;
He watches all who seek.
His unyielding, tender love notes
He gives to each to see.
God built time's own mountains
And ringed them with His seas.
He will reign forever
And forever shall He be.

God is time's firmament glowing
Across the western sky.
God is the raindrops falling
For He is the tears in our eyes.
God is the apple orchard
By which we draw our fruit.
God shall right sustain us
Throughout our family roots.

God is the playful animals
That adorn earth's fragile chest.
God is the One who prods us
to look and do our best.
God never wavers or balks
Upon some turbulous times.
He is strong and unfearful
Through our rhythmic rhymes.

God is like the lily
Nestled by some lake.
God is like the poppy
Growing by some gate.
God is the "Flanders Field"
And all who solemnly lie.
Those who gave their heartthrobs
To them we all should cry.

God is America shining
From sea to shining sea.
God is Old Glory flying
Its stripes for all to see.
God is love and freedom
From out our nation's hope.
God is like the eagle
Soaring as I wrote.

God is evasive action
One must take in time
To assure all foes a'calling
That they had better mind.
God is like the soldier
Guarding America's turf.
God is like the Christ Child
Asleep in His own berth.

God is the divining force
Which sustains me day after day.
He is the challenge a'tuned
That haunts me along life's way.
God is the deepest canyon
Far grander than the Grand.
He is the Earth's floor
Upon which lie life's sand.

God is the smallest kitten
Purring its heart away.
God is the bellowing hound
Which wales of danger's way.
God is the running elk
With antlers tall and wide.
He is the One who gave us
Christ for our own bride.

God is the Master Author
Anointed with timely thoughts.
God is the greatest treasure
Which all men hath so sought.
God is the years a'passing
With wrinkles and aging bones.
God is the lone wolf howling,
Bellowing on and on.

God is the hands so trembling
Scribing out these rhymes.
God is the rhymes a'coming
Line after line after line.
God is the One who seeks us
When death is near the score.
God opens up His mansion
To greet us at His door.

God is everything beautiful
From sea to shining sea.
God is all creation
For which is given so free.
God is the lines a'coming
To poet this darken night.
God is the finished sonnet
That says it, oh, so right.

God is the scrap of paper
Which holds this very rhyme.
God is the thoughts of pen strokes
Embellished throughout all time.
God is the mind a'thinking
Of what to expound on next.
God is the Biblical truths
Throughout His Biblical text.

God is this aging pen stroke
Which scribes this poetic verse.
God is the mind achieving
Thinking of rhyme and verse.
God is the paper proper
Which holds this very thought.
God is the Great Voice
Which says, "What hath I wrought?"

God is the night so lonely
Giving me thoughts to bear.
God is the lamplight shining
To light my pen to share.
God is the age-old prophecy
True and correct in verse.
God is the thoughts a'coming
That never have been rehearsed.

God is the mountains' hilltops
With peaks so cold and white.
God is the valleys deep
Stretching away through this night.
God is the desert glistening
With scrub and cactus plants.
God is the ocean rowing
Drawing our thoughts in trance.

God is the moonbeam raking
Our town this hallowed night.
God is the sun a'shining
Warming our hearts, so right.
God is the field of grass
Which hath a beautiful turf.
God is the scented flower
Which reeks of heavenly myrrh.

William Furr

God is the winter coming
Stocking up His feed,
Not for just the wildlife
But for each of us in need.
God is the brightest aurora
Against the northern sky.
He is fruit of the rapture;
He is the love in our eyes.

God is the breeze a'stirring
From out the western sky.
God is the hurricane going,
Moving in its eye.
God is each our heartthrobs;
For He is all our souls.
He shall not forsake us
Throughout eternity's role.

God is like the forest
With limb and tree and vine.
God is like the aging oak
Full of wisdom's time.
God is wonderful to talk to,
Just go and kneel and pray.
And always spill your heartache
And remember what you say.

God is like the Grand Canyon
Deep and wide in view.
He is large and spacious;
He is there for you.
He is waters flowing
With foam and spume so fast.
Rafting with Him regularly
Will make a Christian last.

God is this rhyme of reason
Telling Christ loves us.
Each and every teardrop
T'was shed from out our worth.
To Him we owe so plenty
To Him we owe our way
Right up the gates of glory
Forever and a day.

God is this day called Sunday;
He is the Son of life
High above our feelings
As we make it through the night.
For if we peer the morrow
And think of our own time
We'll know that God is glory
In rhymic, rhyming lines.

God is earth's cool weather
He is the coming scene
Of snowflakes in some meadow
While "Hark the Herald" sing.
For Christmas tis forth upon us
And we shall surely know
That God paints His new scenery
In a blanket of whitened snow.

God is the bright star shining
Whether planets align or not.
God is all Biblical glory
From David to Noah's ark.
God is the Christ Child cometh
Into our lives to rest
And gather up His children
To reside in heavenly best.

William Furr

God is the early morning
With sunbeams by the way.
God is the call of the lark
Awake, intoned to play.
God is this written demeanor
As He scribbles out His worth.
What I do for Jesus
Shall determine my eternal berth.

God is His rhyme upon me;
He is mine to keep
Way deep down in my poetry
A job, a work, a feat.
For as I pen His message
He shall surely bless
This foolish poet imbedded
With love from out His best.

God is the atom comprising
All matter and elusive space.
God is the bolt of the lightning;
He is the wind in our face.
God is the earth's own minerals
He is the mountain's peak
God shall reign forever
As fools as I doth speak.

God is the time before
To act decisively.
God is His spirit a'moving
Some lost soul to believe.
God is the Holy Ghost
And Christians, oh, so plain.
He is our every wanting
To provide us throughout earth's game.

God is the cup of water
That quenches the thirsty throat.
God is the heavenly manna
The "Bread of Life" unloafed.
God is the fruit in vineyards;
He is the food we see.
He provides us freely
Throughout all eternity.

God is the path so straightly
That stretches through our land.
If we take the "high road"
We'll walk with His own hand.
For we His children forthright
Need to claim His words.
His volumes and volumes of mementos
Are sacred, hallowed verbs.

God is glory hallelujah;
He is the reason we are saved.
God hath freed our shackles
And raised us from the grave.
God hath given me pen strokes
To rhyme what I do best
To tell the world of Jesus
And all the eternal rest.

God is love and goodness;
He is the light of our eyes.
He hath seen our follies
But not to His surprise.
He knows we His children
Are but one rhyme away,
Away from all our play things
We cling to through each day.

God is the love of our neighbor;
He is our very best friend.
God is the sound of children;
He is our peace within.
God is the kinfolk we're sharing.
He is the bride and the groom.
God binds two together
Under the light of the still of the moon.

God gives us His oceans;
He gives us His seas.
And all the fish within
Are there for you and me.
God pulls in His net
And guess what He hath got—
A catch of worldly men
To save from out their lots.

God is the fartherest star glow
From out time's dim-gone past.
God is the all and forever;
He is all that lasts.
God is the fire within me
That continues with this write.
God hath blessed my pen stroke
And prodded me through the night.

God is the forever and forever;
He is that eternal fire
From which is born His creation
And all his love desires.
God is the late night sonnet
That lasts throughout all time.
His shan't ever waiver
From out my rhythmic rhyme.

God is the rain that falleth
From out His skies so high.
God is the Cleansing Redeemer
That washes our sins to die.
God pardons each His children
Those who paid the fees
By asking His forgiveness
Theirs tis heaven to see.

God is the coming Messiah
He shall walk time's road
All the way to Jerusalem
And claim His royal role.
God is the King of His temple
And He shall reign so high
All the way from Bethlehem
And to the eternal sky.

God is the atoms within me
That comprise my very heart.
God is the flesh and the blood flow
Which cause my poem to start.
God is the power within me
To rhyme this world away.
He shall guide my teachings
And lead me all the way.

God is the night that befalls us
When one is taken away.
God is the empty lone chair
As one dies by the way.
He shall give us strength
To continue on His write.
He shall save our souls
And guard us through His night.

God is the power of penning
Writing out his lines
Of poetic prose so freely
Of rhythmic rhyming rhymes.
God is the gift of the lyric
The key to heaven's own gate.
He hath worded his sonnets
And written them on His slate.

God is the fresh night air
That cleanses our minds at rest.
He is the all and forever;
He is the poet's request.
God hath deemed me truly
To expound His own rhyme says
He hath placed my pen stroke
And planned me all the way.

God give me my "Tangy"
My wife of wonderful worth
To prod me on towards glory
And expound what God is worth.
God gave her my mementos
My heart and all my lays.
What I do for Jesus
Shall rhyme and rhyme away.

God gave me the power
The worth within my hand
To tell this world of Jesus
And spread His word to man.
God is all my being
And He is all my heart.
What I do for Jesus
Shall save me from earth's dark.

God is this age upon us
With all its rhyme and stance.
God is this morrow a'lurking
In a poetic rhythmic dance.
God is this rhyme bought freely
Into some heart so true.
God is the Master Poet
In Him I take my cue.

God is this sunny morning
Going off to church.
God is the pastor preaching
His words of Biblical worth.
God is the message expounded
Into our hearts and souls.
God is the Great Provider
As earth doth come of old.

God is the glory of rhyming
Whatever it tis worth
Penning to our Master
His songs throughout this earth.
God is grand and awesome
And forever shall He be
This poet's pen and paper
And all eternity.

God is love unbounded;
He is all and all.
He gives each new poet
His love throughout the fall.
As little do we know
What winter lies ahead,
We pan away His sonnets
Before we lay our heads.

God is the coming deliverance
Of mankind from this earth.
God shall raise us surely
From out our heavenly worth.
He shall give us starlight
And miles and miles to roam.
Once we get to heaven
We'll have a brand-new home.

God is the gift of the lyric
That rhymes and rhymes from birth.
God is the rhythmic rhyme time
That expounds what He is worth.
God is this challenge before me
As I word my poem this night
Praising my own Master
For giving me heaven's new sight.

God is the eternal beauty
Of flowers in His spring.
God is the Everlasting Lord
Of why we call Him King.
God is this late night sonnet
That I pen on and on
Praising my own Master
Before I do my own.

God is creation bountifully
Stretched across His sky.
God is all beauty forever
That man should surely cry.
The awesome love He gave us
Shan't hold us far away.
If we love Him truly,
In heaven we'll live and stay.

God is the tallest pine
Which dwarfs the cedar scrub.
God is the longest vine;
He is the whitest dove.
He is our Lord and Master
And everything I'm told
To fly right up to heaven
And leave this world of old.

God is the fairest brook
Which flows throughout the day.
God is the beautiful meadow
Which stretches along life's way.
He is the luring pull
Of souls and conscience at heart.
He is the colors a'wonder
Which is His work of art.

God is nighttime falling
Upon some hamlet fair
Bedding His own children
To rest their earthly cares.
God is so much matter
That scarce I word my rhyme
Another one comes freely
Through His own chosen lines.

God is birds a'singing
Spelling but His love.
God is what you see
His peaceful high-flying dove.
God is all that matters
Not word on tongue-in-cheek.
God is all forever
To Him we one day meet.

God is the time we have spent
Administering to each man
Each cold and hungry derelict
And Christ and each His clan.
God is the time we have invested
In good and righteous works,
Those things that really matter
And those things of heavenly worth.

God is the center of attention
Of this universe all and large.
God is the pull of gravity
That holds our feet to sod.
God is the changing of seasons
From winter to the spring.
He is the Master Planner,
That's why He is the King.

God is the book on the shelf
Some Bible I've been told.
He is all the verses
Which held our very souls.
He gave us His Genesis
From Revelations to the end;
He has taught us truly
His Word shall never end.

God is the net in time's sea
Pulling man's catch.
He is all our wishes;
He is our eyes that wept.
God is this very poem
Upon which we realize
That rhymes the heavens away
Before our very eyes.

God is the sea breeze blowing
From out the earth's great chest;
God is the long white beachhead
Stretching along earth's crest.
God is the fowl a'flying
Circling our land so free;
God is the coming rapture
To pull us up to He.

God is the teardrops running
Down some sinner's cheeks;
God is the call within us;
He is our souls that speak.
God is the spirit that sends us
Down the church aisle's way;
He is the Holy Spirit
To save us in our days.

God is the lyrics a'flowing
From out this poet at rest;
God is the rhyming rhythm;
He is our zeal and our zest.
God is the continuous prelude
That comes before we pray;
God is the fire within us
To light our heavenly way.

God is the tree a'standing
With limbs outstretching with glee;
God is the branch a'moving
For you and I to see.
God is the late night raindrop;
He is the coming storm.
God shall send His Son
To guide, protect and warn.

William Furr

God is the day upon us
With sky and sea and land;
God is the mighty high cloud
Stretching along earth's realm.
God is the lush green valley
So full of life at best;
His is the glow of sunlight
To guide us in our quest.

God is the age of workers
Each, in his every right;
God is the labor a'toiling
Building his life tonight.
As we stack each brick form
And lay our eternal plans
We shall find our glory
Far from earthly man.

God is the deep swamp bottom
Full of fish and prey;
God is the thickest forest
From which we lose our way.
God is the span of dessert;
He is the trickling brook;
God is my heart within me
Which cries to write a book.

God is the longest poem
Which tells of what we word;
God is the love that sung it
As if to say in verbs.
All those cherished moments
And all those heartful lays
Each shall find their solace
From out the Milky Way.

God is the late night sonnet
Rhyming our lives away;
God is this poet a'yearning
For love as He writes His say.
God is this stark white paper
From which my ink shall run;
God is the lyrics a'rhyming
As thoughts and melodies come.

God is the pen I'm holding
As lyrics escape with rhyme;
God is the stanza singing
Which tells of Christ divine.
God is the brain within me
Which computes in earthly jest;
All those lines within me
Somehow they rhyme their best.

God is the newborn baby
Alive and heavenly sweet;
God is the freshest rosebud
Its beauty an awesome feat.
God is the oil on the canvas
Drying from out a toil;
God is the coming star beam
From which I word my spoils.

God is the aging graveyard
Which holds our kin this day;
God is the marker standing
Adorning our ones that lay.
God is the church bell ringing
Telling of those that passed;
God is the love that left us
When our true one hath lapsed.

God is the coming Rapture
By which we'll leave this earth;
God is the hour upon us
To find our heavenly berth.
God is the awesome star light
Which bathes those heavenly gates
For all who rightly seek them
Jesus shall patiently wait.

God is the moving pendulum
Which ticks earth's hours away;
God is the hour a'plenty
For He shall show the way.
God draws each His children
To Him in heavenly prayer;
God shall born tomorrow
And banish our earthly cares.

God is the eagle a'soaring
High above earth's rain;
God is the torrents pouring
To cleanse this earth of pain.
God is the deer a'flocking
In meadow and heavenly clover;
God is the time we're spending
To look our souls right over.

God is the tune of love songs;
He is the bride and the prince.
God is the Rock of Gibraltar;
He is the Christ whom He sent.
God is the mastermind cometh;
He is the rhyme that hath ran.
God shall move we Christians
And silence all sinful man.

God is the Ark of the Covenant;
He is the fire and the flame.
God hath moved His starlight
To each who play time's game.
God shall spend His wise time
Loving and saving just me;
He hath paved tomorrow
And blessed us endlessly.

God is this fool of a poet
Who toils just night after night.
God is the fire within us;
He is the one who hath might.
God is the true words coming
To admonish all earthly man;
God hath made creation
And given us Jesus' hand.

God is the moving emotion
Which grips our hearts so strong;
God is the teardrop running
As we turn our thoughts towards home.
God is the warmth within us
As we think of Christ, our King;
God is the hour upon us
As we lift our voice to sing.

God is the ban of angels
Which guards our souls at rest;
God is the love He Gave us
As our hearts, now open, confess.
God is that hallowed promise
Given many years hence gone
That all who earnestly seek Christ
Shall find their eternal home.

William Furr

God is the voice from the heavens
That warns when danger's nigh;
God is the fawn in the forest
Finding a place to lie.
God is the ship on the ocean
Tossed in turbulent seas;
God shall still the water
And draw our souls to He.

God is the rhymes a'coming
Singing what Christ hath done;
God is the promise made us
As His hourglass doth run.
God is this writer a'toiling
Night after night after night;
God is this poet's heartstrings
Putting his thoughts to sight.

God is the pen now writing
These words so moving with time;
God is the sonnet that cometh
And leaps from the heart sublime.
God is the thought that careth
And plays time's memorable words;
God is the poet now sitting
Drawing his sacred verbs.

God is the sky so brilliant
Where larks doth endlessly soar;
God is the fringe of spacetime
With heaven's wide open door.
God is the fire within us
The torch that lights the world;
God is the moving finger
Drawing eternity's words.

God is the pendulum swinging
Moving fro with time;
God is the hours a'passing
In a host of rhythmic rhymes.
God is the time upon us
When we shall truly mark
Eternity's awesome endings
They, hence, shall never start.

God is the Christmas season
Which glorifies the One;
God is the gift of giving
For Christ hath truly won.
God is the pen I'm holding
Spelling out my rhyme;
Tis a gift from the Master
Which I hath claimed for mine.

God is the quiet night hour
As minutes come and pass;
God is the poet a'toiling
Writing His thoughts at last.
God is the south wind blowing
Melting His fallen snow;
God is each and everything
This lesson we need to know.

God is the beggar holding
His cupful of pens;
God is the blind man singing
For Jesus to come right in.
God is the cold in the morning;
He is the warmth of the night.
For all who rightly seek Him
Shall find their hearts tonight.

God is the fresh found clover
Stretching along life's way;
He is the dew on the daisies
That frolics this new-found May.
God is the little small greenery
That grows up from His sod;
He hath made the meadow
Adorned with golden rod.

God is the flow from His fountain
That all who drinks shall last.
God is the cup of His vineyard;
He is the sun we hath basked.
God shall surely let us
Enter unto His great hall
Those castles of pearly gold filled
Just beyond His gate and His wall.

God is the mighty explosion
By which He casts His stars.
God is the ranging heavens
Which say "how great Thou art."
God is the all and forever
And eternal shall He be
Time's great, compassionate Master
Who loves us endlessly!

The End

About the Author

Poetry brings emotions to the surface. In this book you will find a wonderful selection of deeply emotional, eloquently written poetry. These beautiful rhymes and moving tenets will give the reader the opportunity to understand the real William Furr.

William has faced many challenges in his lifetime. He began life in Columbus, MS on August 6th, 1945. This date was important to William as this is also the birth date of the famous poet Alfred Lord Tennyson.

Before William was one year of age, he had to undergo surgery. This surgery caused complications with his breathing and William died on the operating table. The technology was not as sophisticated as it is today. However, they were able to revive William, although he was without oxygen long enough for his skin to discolor.

William also fell from a second-story balcony when he was a small boy. He landed head first on a brick terrace and required medical treatment. As William grew into a young man, he began noticing problems with concentrating. Words of rhyme continued to flow through his mind. He could not stop them. As schizophrenia set in, the obsessive compulsive disorder became full blown. High school was a real challenge because of his mental health, and William was only able to finish the 8th grade.

Despite all of these problems and lack of formal education, William is a master at composition. He regularly corresponds with some of the most influential people around the world. William has received personal letters from Pope John Paul II, President Bush, Queen Elizabeth, Yitzhak Shamire, Hosni Morbarak, Carlos Salinas, Francois Mitterand, and many more. William has been the featured speaker at Universities and sat on many advisory boards.

He is a very versatile author who composes poetry, songs and short stories. The Honorable G. V. " Sonny" Montgomery published William's poem "Salute to the Heroes" in the Congressional Record.

As you lose yourself in his wandering tales, consider the mental state of the author. William continues to suffer from both schizophrenia and obsessive compulsive disorder. One wonders how someone so fraught with mental disease could concentrate enough to write exquisitely beautiful prose. Please keep this in mind as you step into his alluring words....

Printed in the United States
136064LV00004B/2/A

9 781420 870534